REFERENCE GUIDES IN AMERICAN LITERATURE
Joseph Katz, General Editor
SYLVIA PLATH AND ANNE SEXTON. NO. 1

SYLVIA PLATH
AND ANNE SEXTON:
A REFERENCE GUIDE

Cameron Northouse
Thomas P. Walsh

G. K. HALL & CO., 70 LINCOLN STREET, BOSTON, MASS. 1974

79-359

Library of Congress Cataloging in Publication Data

Northouse, Cameron.
   Sylvia Plath and Anne Sexton: a reference guide.

   (Reference guides in American literature, no. 1)
    1. Plath, Sylvia--Bibliography. 2. Sexton, Anne--
Bibliography. I. Walsh, Thomas P., joint author.
II. Title.
Z8695.85.N67   016.811'5'4   74-14965
ISBN 0-8161-1146-4

Preface

It is easy to talk about Anne Sexton and Sylvia Plath together. Both poets are concerned with the same general subject: incoherence between self and object, and the chaos that grows out of that incoherence. Both poets published their first book in 1960. Both were strongly influenced by Robert Lowell, and both have received a mixed critical reaction. At times they both were condemned for writing what was interpreted as weak, exhibitionist verse that seemed to trade on an exaggeration of personal tragedy; at other times they were praised for writing poetry that speaks to the modern condition with profundity and insight.

Despite the convergence of their careers, Plath and Sexton were of course individuals. Until her death in 1963, Plath received a modicum of critical praise for her work; but it was not until 1965, when Ariel appeared posthumously, that much began to be written about her. In terms of that comment, Ariel must be considered one of the most important works of poetry in recent years. Writings about Sexton have been more moderate in bulk, and in their relative slimness they tend much more to quite different estimates of the worth of her work. Certainly, none of her books has influenced contemporary poetry in the manner of Ariel. Nevertheless, Sexton and Plath are frequently compared, with Sexton's work considered derivative.

This Reference Guide to Sylvia Plath and Anne Sexton is divided into two sections, one on each poet.

PREFACE

Each section has the same structure and intent. The
first part lists their work, in chronological order of
publication. The second part records the major writings
we have found about them, again in chronological order
of publication. Within those second sections we have
subdivided the listing for each year into "A. Books"
and "B. Articles" ("articles" should be understood to
include also parts of books not exclusively on the
poet). Arrangement within each year is alphabetical,
by author. All entries in the second sections are
annotated with a brief abstract of the content of the
work. We tried to see the original appearance of
everything we list. In the relatively few instances
where we did not succeed and had to use a reprinting,
we follow the bibliographic listing with an asterisk
(*) and include in the annotation a note on our source
of the work. The part of this book on Sylvia Plath
attempts to be comprehensive through 1972, with items
we have found in 1973 also included. The part on Anne
Sexton attempts comprehensiveness through 1971. There
are separate indexes to each part of this book.

Contents

Writings by Sylvia Plath

Prose--1952

1 "Sunday at the Minton's." _Mademoiselle_, XXXV
   (August, 1952), 255, 371-378

2 "Sunday at the Minton's." _Smith Review_ (Fall,
   1952), 3-9

Prose--1953

1 "Poet's On Campus." _Mademoiselle_, XXXVII (August,
   1953), 290-291

2 "Mademoiselle's Last Word on College." _Mademoiselle_,
   XXXVII (August, 1953), 235

Poetry--1953

1 "Mad Girl's Lovesong." _Smith Review_ (Spring, 1953),
   13

2 "To Eva Descending the Stairs." _Smith Review_
   (Spring, 1953), 22

3 "Doomsday." _Smith Review_ (Spring, 1953), 22

4 "Mad Girl's Lovesong." _Mademoiselle_, XXXVIII
   (August, 1953), 358

BY SYLVIA PLATH (1954)

Prose--1954

1 "In the Mountains." Smith Review (Fall, 1954), 2-5

Poetry--1954

1 "Doomsday." Harper's, CCVIII (May, 1954), 29

2 "Denouement." Smith Review (Spring, 1954), 23

3 "Admonition." Smith Review (Spring, 1954), 23

4 "To Eva Descending the Stairs." Harper's, CCIX
   (September, 1954), 63

5 "Circus in Three Rings." Smith Review (Fall, 1954),
   18

6 "Go Get the Goodly Squab." Harper's CCIX (November,
   1954), 47

Prose--1955

1 "Superman and Paula Brow's New Snowsuit." Smith
   Review (Spring, 1955), 19-21

Poetry--1955

1 "Dialogue en Route." Smith Review (January, 1955),
   12

2 "Danse Macabre." Smith Review (Spring, 1955), 12

3 "Temper of Time." Nation, CLXXI (August 6, 1955),
   119

BY SYLVIA PLATH (1955)

4   "Two Lovers and a Beachcomber by the Sea." <u>Made-moiselle</u>, XLI (August, 1955), 52

5   "Circus in Three Rings." <u>Atlantic</u>, CXCVI (August, 1955), 68

6   "Lament." <u>New Orleans Poetry Journal</u>, I (October, 1955), 19

Prose--1956

1   "The Day Mr. Prescott Died." <u>Granta</u>, LX (October 20, 1956), 20-23

Poetry--1956

1   "Sketchbook of a Spanish Summer." <u>Christian Science Monitor</u> (November 5, 1956), p.13

2   "Apotheosis." <u>Lyric</u>, I (Winter, 1956), 10

3   "Second Winter." <u>Lyric</u>, I (Winter, 1956), 11

Prose--1957

1   "The Wishing Box." <u>Granta</u>, LXI (January 26, 1957), 3-5

Poetry--1957

1   "Wreath for a Bridal." <u>Poetry</u>, LXXXIX (January, 1957), 231

2   "Dream With Clam-Diggers." <u>Poetry</u>, LXXXIX (January, 1957), 232-233

BY SYLVIA PLATH (1957)

3 "Strumpet Song." Poetry, LXXXIX (January, 1957),
     233

4 "Metamorphosis." Poetry, LXXXIX (January, 1957),
     234

5 "Two Sisters of Persephone." Poetry (January, 1957),
     235-236

6 "Epitaph for Fire and Flowers." Poetry, LXXXIX
     (January, 1957), 237

7 "Pursuit." Atlantic, XCIX (January, 1957), 65

8 "Two Lovers and a Beachcomber by the Real Sea."
     Granta, LXI (March 9, 1957), 5

9 "Resolve." Granta, LXI (March 9, 1957), 5

10 "Mad Girl's Lovesong." Granta, LXI (May 4, 1957),
      19

11 "Soliloquy of the Solipsist." Granta, LXI (May 4,
      1957), 19

12 "Black Rook in Rainy Weather." Granta, LXI (May 18,
      1957), 9

13 "The Snowman on the Moor." Poetry, XC (July, 1957),
      229-231

14 "Sow." Poetry, XC (July, 1957), 231-232

15 "Ella Mason and Her Eleven Cats." Poetry, XC
      (July, 1957), 232-234

16 "On the Difficulty of Conjuring Up a Dryad."
      Poetry, XC (July, 1957), 235-236

BY SYLVIA PLATH (1957)

17 "Black Rook in Rainy Weather." Antioch Review,
       CVII (Summer, 1957), 232-233

18 "Recantation." Accent, XVII (Autumn, 1957), 247

19 "Tinker Jack and the Tidy Wives." Accent, XVII
       (Autumn, 1957), 247

20 "On the Plethora of Dryads." New Mexico Quarterly,
       XXVII (Autumn, 1957), 211-212

21 "All the Dead Dears." Grecourt Review, I (November,
       1957), 36-37

Poetry--1958

1 "Spinster." London Magazine, V (June, 1958), 46-47

2 "Black Rook in Rainy Weather." London Magazine, V
       (June, 1958), 47-48

3 "Mussel Hunter at Rock Harbor." New Yorker, XXXIV
       (August 9, 1958), 22

4 "Night Walk." New Yorker, XXXIV (October 11, 1958),

5 "Second Winter." Ladies Home Journal, LXXV (Decem-
       ber, 1958), 143

Poetry--1959

1 "Frog Autumn." Nation, CLXXXVIII (January 24, 1959),
       74

2 "Companionable Ills." Spectator, CCII (January 30,
       1959), 163

BY SYLVIA PLATH (1959)

3 "The Times Are Tidy." Mademoiselle, XLVIII (January, 1959), 34

4 "Main Street at Midnight." Spectator, CCII (February 13, 1959), 227

5 "Departure." Nation, CLXXXVIII (March 7, 1959), 212

6 "Prologue to Spring." Christian Science Monitor (March 26, 1959), p.8

7 "'Yadwigha on a Red Couch, Among Lilies' (A Sestina for the Douanier)." Christian Science Monitor (March 26, 1959), p.8

8 "Snakecharmer." London Magazine, VI (March, 1959), 33-34

9 "Lorelei." London Magazine, VI (March, 1959), 34-35

10 "The Disquieting Muses." London Magazine, VI (March, 1959), 35-36

11 "The Bull of Bendylaw." Hornbook, XXXV (April, 1959), 148

12 "Sculptor." Grécourt Review, II (May, 1959), 282

13 "Lorelei." Audience, VI (Spring, 1959), 33

14 "Full Fathom Five." Audience, VI (Spring, 1959), 34-35

15 "The Hermit of Outermost House." Audience, VI (Spring, 1959), 36

16 "Fiesta Melons." Christian Science Monitor (July 31, 1959), p.8

BY SYLVIA PLATH (1959)

17 "Song for Summer Day." Christian Science Monitor
     (August 18, 1959), p.8

18 "Southern Sunrise." Christian Science Monitor
     (August 26, 1959), p.8

19 "The Departure of the Ghost." Sewanee Review,
     LXVII (Summer, 1959), 446-447

20 "Point Shirley." Sewanee Review, LXVII (Summer,
     1959), 447-448

21 "On the Decline of Oracles." Poetry, XCVI (Septem-
     ber, 1959), 368-369

22 "The Death of Mythmaking." Poetry, XCVI (September,
     1959), 370

23 "A Lesson in Vengeance." Poetry, XCVI (September,
     1959), 371

24 "In Midas Country." London Magazine, VI (October,
     1959), 11

25 "The Thin People." London Magazine, VI (October,
     1959), 12-13

26 "I Want, I Want." Partisan Review, XXVI (Fall,
     1959), 558

27 "Aftermath." Arts in Society, (Fall, 1966), 66

28 "The Goring." Arts in Society, (Fall, 1966), 66

29 "Sculptor." Arts in Society, (Fall, 1966), 67

30 "Two Views of a Cadaver Room." London Times
     Literary Supplement (November 6, 1959), p.xxiii

BY SYLVIA PLATH (1959)

31 "The Hermit of Outermost House." London Times
    Literary Supplement (November 6, 1959), p.xxiv

32 "Winter's Tale." New Yorker, XXXV (December 12,
    1959), 116

Books--1960

1 The Colossus and Other Poems. London: Heinemann,
   1960. New York: Alfred Knopf, 1962. London:
   Faber and Faber, 1967

Prose--1960

1 "The Daughters of Blossom Street." London Magazine,
   VII (May, 1960), 34-48

2 "Fifteen Dollar Eagle." Sewanee Review, LXVIII
   (Fall, 1960), 603-618

Poetry--1960

1 "Two Views of a Cadaver Room." Nation, CXC (January 30, 1960), 107

2 "Man in Black." New Yorker, XXXVI (April 9, 1960),
   40

3 "Watercolor of Grantchester Meadows." New Yorker,
   XXXVI (May 28, 1960), 30

4 "The Beggars." Chelsea Review, VII (May, 1960), 70

5 "The Eye-Mote." Chelsea Review, VII (May, 1960), 71

BY SYLVIA PLATH (1960)

6   "The Sleepers." London Magazine, VII (June, 1960), 11

7   "Full Fathom Five." London Magazine, VII (June, 1960), 12-13

8   "A Winter Ship." Atlantic, CCVI (July, 1960), 65

9   "Mushrooms." Harper's, CCXXI (July, 1960), 25

10 "The Net Menders." New Yorker, XXXVI (August 20, 1960), 36

11 "The Manor Garden." Critical Quarterly, II (Summer, 1960), 155

12 "The Beggars." Critical Quarterly, II (Summer, 1960), 156

13 "Blue Moles." Critical Quarterly, II (Summer, 1960), 156-157

14 "Metaphors for a Pregnant Woman." Partisan Review, XXVII (Summer, 1960), 435

15 "The Manor Garden." Atlantic, CCVI (September, 1960), 52

16 "Ouija." Hudson Review, XIII (Autumn, 1960), 413

17 "Electra on the Azalea Path." Hudson Review, XIII (Autumn, 1960), 414-415

18 "Suicide Off Egg Rock." Hudson Review, XIII (Autumn, 1960), 415

19 "Moonrise." Hudson Review, XIII (Autumn, 1960), 416

BY SYLVIA PLATH (1960)

20 "The Beekeeper's Daughter." Kenyon Review, XXII
      (Fall, 1960), 595

21 "The Colossus." Kenyon Review, XXII (Fall, 1960),
      596

22 "Candles." Listener, LXIV (November 17, 1960), 877

23 "Flute Notes From a Reedy Pond." Texas Quarterly,
      III (Winter, 1960), 120

24 "Hardcastle Crags" in The Golden Year: The Poetry
      Society of America Anthology 1910-1960. Ed.
      Melville Crane, et al. New York: Fine Editions
      Press, 1960, 220-221

25 "Two Views of a Cadaver Room" in The Golden Year:
      The Poetry Society of America Anthology 1910-
      1960. Ed. Melville Crane, et al. New York:
      Fine Editions Press, 1960, 219-220

Books--1961

1 Sylvia Plath, ed. American Poetry Now: Critical
      Quarterly Poetry Supplement Number Two, 1961

Prose--1961

1 "The Fifty-Ninth Bear." London Magazine, VIII
      (February, 1961), 11-20

Poetry--1961

1 "A Winter Ship." Encounter, XVI (February, 1961),
      23

BY SYLVIA PLATH (1961)

2 "Magi." New Statesman, LXI (March 31, 1961), 514

3 "A Life." Listener, LXV (May 4, 1961), 776

4 "You're." Harper's, CCXXII (June, 1961), 40

5 "On Deck." New Yorker, XXXVII (July 22, 1961), 32

6 "Words for a Nursery." Atlantic, CCVIII (August, 1961), 66

7 "Zoo Keeper's Wife." London Magazine, I (August, 1961), 5-6

8 "You're." London Magazine, I (August, 1961), 6

9 "Small Hours." London Magazine, I (August, 1961), 7

10 "Parliament Hill Fields." London Magazine, I (August, 1961), 7-8

11 "Whitsun." London Magazine, I (August, 1961), 9

12 "Leaving Early." London Magazine, I (August, 1961), 9-10

13 "Private Ground." Critical Quarterly, III (Summer, 1961), pp.140-141

14 "I Am Vertical." Critical Quarterly, III (Summer, 1961), p.140

15 "Witch Burning." Texas Quarterly, IV (Autumn, 1961), 84

16 "Mojave Desert." London Observer (November 19, 1961), p.28

BY SYLVIA PLATH (1961)

17 "Insomniac." <u>Cheltenham Festival Programme</u>. Cheltenham, 1961

Prose--1962

1 "Context." <u>London Magazine</u>, I (February, 1962), 45-46

2 "Oblongs." <u>New Statesman</u>, LXIII (May 18, 1962), 724

3 "Pair of Queens." <u>New Statesman</u>, LXIII (May 18, 1962), 724

Poetry--1962

1 "The Rival." <u>London Observer</u> (January 21, 1962), p.31

2 "In Plaster." <u>London Magazine</u>, I (February, 1962), 15-17

3 "Sleep in the Mojave Desert." <u>Harper's</u>, CCXXIV (February, 1962), 36

4 "Wuthering Heights." <u>New Statesman</u>, LXIII (March 16, 1962), 390

5 "Stars Over Dordogne." <u>Poetry</u>, XCIX (March, 1962), 346-347

6 "Widow." <u>Poetry</u>, XCIX (March, 1962), 347-348

7 "Face Lift." <u>Poetry</u>, XCIX (March, 1962), 349

8 "Heavy Woman." <u>Poetry</u>, XCIX (March, 1962), 350

BY SYLVIA PLATH (1962)

9 "Love Letter." Poetry, XCIX (March, 1962), 350-351

10 "Tulips." New Yorker, XXXVIII (April 7, 1962), 40

11 "The Colossus." Encounter, XVIII (April, 1962), 56

12 "Finisterre." London Observer (August 5, 1962),
      p.14

13 "Private Ground." Harper's, CCXXV (August, 1962),
      55

14 "Blackberrying." New Yorker, XXXVIII (September 15,
      1962), 48

15 "The Surgeon at 2 A.M." Listener, LXVIII (September
      20, 1962), 428

16 "Crossing the Water." London Observer (September
      23, 1962), p.25

17 "Event." London Observer (December 16, 1962), p.21

18 "Leaving Early." Harper's, CCXXV (December, 1962),
      82

19 "Parliament Hill Fields." Critical Quarterly Poetry
      Supplement Number Three, 1962, 10

20 "Lady Lazarus" in The New Poetry. Ed. A. Alvarez.
      Harmondsworth: Penguin Brooks, 1962, 61-64

21 "Daddy" in The New Poetry. Ed. A. Alvarez. Har-
      mondsworth: Penguin Brooks, 1962, 64-66

22 "The Moon and the Yew Tree" in The New Poetry. Ed.
      A. Alvarez. Harmondsworth: Penguin Brooks,
      1962, 66-67

BY SYLVIA PLATH (1962)

23 "The Arrival of the Bee Box" in The New Poetry. Ed.
      A. Alvarez. Harmondsworth: Penguin Books, 1962,
      67-68

24 "The Swarm" in The New Poetry. Ed. A. Alvarez.
      Harmondsworth: Penguin Books, 1962, 69-71

25 "Childless Woman" in The New Poetry. Ed. A. Alvarez.
      Harmondsworth: Penguin Books, 1962, 71

26 "Mary's Song" in The New Poetry. Ed. A. Alvarez.
      Harmondsworth: Penguin Books, 1962, 72

Books--1963

1 The Bell Jar. (By "Victoria Lucas.") London:
      Heinemann, 1963. (By Sylvia Plath.) London:
      Faber and Faber, 1966. New York: Harper and
      Row, 1971

Prose--1963

1 "Ocean 1212-W." Listener, LXX (August 29, 1963),
      312-313

Poetry--1963

1 "Stopped Dead." London Magazine, II (January,
      1963), 14-15

2 "The Applicant." London Magazine, II (January,
      1963), 15-16

3 "Contusion." London Observer (February 17, 1963),
      p.23

BY SYLVIA PLATH (1963)

4 "Edge." London Observer (February 17, 1963), p.23

5 "The Fearful." London Observer (February 17, 1963),
      p.23

6 "Kindness." London Observer (February 17, 1963),
      p.23

7 "The Bee Meeting." London Magazine, III (April,
      1963), 24-25

8 "Stings." London Magazine, III (April, 1963), 26-27

9 "Cut." London Magazine, III (April, 1963), 28-29

10 "Letter in November." London Magazine, III (April,
      1963), 29-30

11 "The Couriers." London Magazine, III (April, 1963),
      30-31

12 "Mary's Song." London Magazine, III (April, 1963),
      31

13 "Years." London Magazine, III (April, 1963), 32

14 "The Arrival of the Bee Box." Atlantic, CCXI
      (April, 1963), 70

15 "Wintering." Atlantic, CCXI (April, 1963), 70-71

16 "Child." New Statesman, LXV (May 31, 1963), 683

17 "A Birthday Present." Critical Quarterly, V
      (Spring, 1963), 3-4

18 "The Elm Speaks." New Yorker, XXXIX (August 3,
      1963), 28

BY SYLVIA PLATH (1963)

19 "Two Campers in Cloud Country." <u>New Yorker</u>, XXXIX (August 3, 1963), 28

20 "Mystic." <u>New Yorker</u>, XXXIX (August 3, 1963), 28-29

21 "Amnesiac." <u>New Yorker</u>, XXXIX (August 3, 1963), 29

22 "Mirror." <u>New Yorker</u>, XXXIX (August 3, 1963), 29

23 "Among the Narcissi." <u>New Yorker</u>, XXXIX (August 3, 1963), 29

24 "The Moon and the Yew Tree." <u>New Yorker</u>, XXXIX (August 3, 1963), 29

25 "Fever 103°." <u>Poetry</u>, CII (August, 1963), 292-294

26 "Purdah." <u>Poetry</u>, CII (August, 1963), 294-296

27 "Eavesdropper." <u>Poetry</u>, CII (August, 1963), 296-298

28 "For a Fatherless Son." <u>Critical Quarterly</u>, V (Summer, 1963), 115

29 "Poppies in October." <u>London Observer</u> (October 6, 1963), p.24

30 "Death & Co." <u>Encounter</u>, XXI (October, 1963), 45

31 "The Swarm." <u>Encounter</u>, XXI (October, 1963), 45-46

32 "The Other." <u>Encounter</u>, XXI (October, 1963), 47

33 "Getting There." <u>Encounter</u>, XXI (October, 1963), 47-48

BY SYLVIA PLATH (1963)

34 "Lady Lazarus." Encounter, XXI (October, 1963), 49

35 "Little Fugue." Encounter, XXI (October, 1963), 50

36 "Childless Woman." Encounter, XXI (October, 1963),
       50

37 "The Jailer." Encounter, XXI (October, 1963), 51

38 "Thalidomide." Encounter, XXI (October, 1963), 51

39 "Daddy." Encounter, XXI (October, 1963), 52

40 "Daddy." The Review, 9 (October, 1963), 4-6

41 "Lady Lazarus." The Review, 9 (October, 1963), 7-9

42 "Fever 103°." The Review, 9 (October, 1963), 10-11

43 "Ariel." The Review, 9 (October, 1963), 12

44 "Poppies in October." The Review, 9 (October, 1963),
       13

45 "Nick and the Candlestick." The Review, 9 (October,
       1963), 13-14

46 "Brasilia." The Review, 9 (October, 1963), 15

47 "Mary's Song." The Review, 9 (October, 1963), 16

48 "Lesbos." The Review, 9 (October, 1963), 17-19

49 "The Horse." London Observer (November 3, 1963), 22

Prose--1964

 1 "The Wishing Box." Atlantic, CCXIV (October, 1964),
       86-89

BY SYLVIA PLATH (1964)

Poetry--1964

1 "Small Hours." Critical Quarterly Supplement Number
Five (1964), 2

2 "In Plaster." Critical Quarterly Supplement Number
Five (1964), 3-4

Books--1965

1 Ariel. London: Faber and Faber, 1965. New York:
Harper and Row, 1966

2 Uncollected Poems. London: Turret Press, 1965

Poetry--1965

1 "November Graveyard." Mademoiselle, LXII (November
1965), 134

2 "The Bee Meeting." Critical Quarterly Supplement
Number Six (1965), 2-3

3 "Lady Lazarus." Critical Quarterly Supplement Number Six (1965), 3-5

Poetry--1966

1 "An Appearance." London Times Literary Supplement
(January 20, 1966), p.42

2 "Daddy." Time, LXXXVII (June 10, 1966), 118

3 "The Death of Myth-Making." Tri-Quarterly, 7 (Fall,
1966), 11

BY SYLVIA PLATH (1966)

4   "Sow." _Tri-Quarterly_, 7 (Fall, 1966), 11-12

5   "Watercolor of Grantchester Meadows." _Tri-Quarterly_, 7 (Fall, 1966), 13

6   "The Colossus." _Tri-Quarterly_, 7 (Fall, 1966), 14

7   "Mushrooms." _Tri-Quarterly_, 7 (Fall, 1966), 15

8   "Sculptor." _Tri-Quarterly_, 7 (Fall, 1966), 16

9   "In Plaster." _Tri-Quarterly_, 7 (Fall, 1966), 16-17

10 "Lesbos." _Tri-Quarterly_, 7 (Fall, 1966), 18-20

11 "Words For a Nursery." _Tri-Quarterly_, 7 (Fall, 1966), 21

12 "Nick and the Candlestick." _Tri-Quarterly_, 7 (Fall, 1966), 22-23

13 "Stings." _Tri-Quarterly_, 7 (Fall, 1966), 24-25

14 "Fever 103°." _Tri-Quarterly_, 7 (Fall, 1966), 26-27

15 "Cut." _Tri-Quarterly_, 7 (Fall, 1966), 28

16 "The Bee Meeting." _Tri-Quarterly_, 7 (Fall, 1966), 29-30

17 "Death & Co." _Tri-Quarterly_, 7 (Fall, 1966), 31

18 "Daddy." _Tri-Quarterly_, 7 (Fall, 1966), 32-34

19 "Lady Lazarus." _Tri-Quarterly_, 7 (Fall, 1966), 35-37

20 "Words." _Tri-Quarterly_, 7 (Fall, 1966), 38

BY SYLVIA PLATH (1967)

Poetry--1967

1 "Mad Girl's Love Song." Harvard Advocate, CI (May, 1967), 2-3

2 "Admonition." Harvard Advocate, CI (May, 1967), 2-3

3 "Circus in Three Rings." Harvard Advocate, CI (May, 1967), 2-3

4 "Dialogue en Route." Harvard Advocate, CI (May, 1967), 2-3

5 "Danse Macabre." Harvard Advocate, CI (May, 1967), 2-3

Books--1968

1 Three Women. London: Turret Press, 1968

Prose--1968

1 "Johnny Panic and the Bible of Dreams." Atlantic, CCXXII (September, 1968), 54-60

Poetry--1968

1 "Two Poems." Critical Quarterly, X (Autumn, 1968), 213-214. (Excerpt from Three Women.)

2 "Extract from 'Three Women, A Radio Play.'" Trans-atlantic Review, 31 (Winter, 1968-1969), 51-52

BY SYLVIA PLATH (1969)

Poetry--1969

1 "Street Song." Cambridge Review, XC (February 7, 1969), 244

2 "Aerialist." Cambridge Review, XC (February 7, 1969), 245

3 "Complaint of the Crazed Queen." London Times Literary Supplement (July 31, 1969), p.855

4 "Battle-Scene From the Comic Operatic Fantasy 'The Seafarer.'" London Times Literary Supplement (July 31, 1969), p.855

5 "Letter to a Purist." London Times Literary Supplement (July 31, 1969), p.855

6 "Dream of the Hearse Driver." London Times Literary Supplement (July 31, 1969), p.855

7 "From 'Three Women, A Radio Play.'" Quarterly Review of Literature, XVI (1969), 197-198

Books--1970

1 Wreath For A Bridal. Frensham: Sceptre Press, 1970

Poetry--1970

1 "Lyonesse." London Observer (May 10, 1970), p.31

2 "Two Campers in Cloud Country." Critical Quarterly, XII (Summer, 1970), 149

3 "On Deck." Critical Quarterly, XII (Summer, 1970), 150

BY SYLVIA PLATH (1970)

4 "Gigolo." New Yorker, XLVI (November 21, 1970), 54

Books--1971

1 Crossing the Water. London: Faber and Faber, 1971
     New York: Harper and Row. 1972

2 Crystal Gazer. London: Rainbow Press, 1971

3 Lyonnesse. London: Rainbow Press, 1971

4 Million Dollar Month. Frensham: Sceptre Press, 1971

5 Winter Trees. London: Faber and Faber, 1971. New
     York: Harper and Row, 1972

Prose--1971

1 "What I Found Out About Buddy Willard." McCall's,
     XCVIII (April, 1971), 86-87. (Excerpt from The
     Bell Jar.)

2 "The Fifty-Ninth Bear" in Works in Progress. Ed.
     Martha Saxton. New York: Literary Guild, 1971,
     17-31

Poetry--1971

1 "Babysitters." New Yorker, XLVII (March 6, 1971),
     36

2 "Pheasant." New Yorker, XLVII (March 6, 1971), 36

3 "The Courage of Shutting Up." New Yorker, XLVII
     (March 6, 1971), 36-37

BY SYLVIA PLATH (1971)

4   "Apprehensions." New Yorker, XLVII (March 6, 1971), 37

5   "For a Fatherless Son." New Yorker, XLVII (March 6, 1971), 37

6   "By Candlelight." New Yorker, XLVII (March 6, 1971), 37

7   "Stillborn." New Statesman, LXXXI (March 19, 1971), 384

8   "Tour." London Times Literary Supplement (May 28, 1971), p.610

9   "The Courage of Shutting Up." London Magazine, XI (September, 1971), 41-42

10 "For a Fatherless Son." London Magazine, XI (September, 1971), 42-43

11 "By Candlelight." London Magazine, XI (September, 1971), 44-45

12 "Gigolo." London Magazine, XI (September, 1971), 45-46

13 "Crossing the Water." Intellectual Digest, II (November, 1971), 95

14 "Lady Lazarus." Intellectual Digest, II (November, 1971), 95

15 "Edge." Intellectual Digest, II (November, 1971), 95

16 "The Complaint of the Crazed Queen" in Works in Progress. Ed. Martha Saxton. New York: Literary Guild, 1971, 11-12

BY SYLVIA PLATH (1971)

17 "Battle-Scene From the Comic Operatic Fantasy 'The Seafarer'" in <u>Works in Progress</u>. Ed. Martha Saxton. New York: Literary Guild, 1971, 13-14

18 "Letter to a Purist" in <u>Works in Progress</u>. Ed. Martha Saxton. New York: Literary Guild, 1971, 15

19 "Dream of the Hearse Driver" in <u>Works in Progress</u>. Ed. Martha Saxton. New York: Literary Guild, 1971, 16

Prose--1972

1 "Mother's Union." <u>McCall's</u>, C (October, 1972), 80-81

Poetry--1972

1 "Stopped Dead." <u>Mademoiselle</u>, LXXIV (March, 1972), 30

2 "Winter Trees." <u>Mademoiselle</u>, LXXIV (March, 1972), 30

3 "Three Women: A Poem For Three Voices." <u>Ms</u>., I (Spring, 1972), 85-88

4 "Metamorphosis." <u>Poetry</u>, CXXI (October, 1972), 25

Poetry--1973

1 "Morning Song." <u>Redbook</u>, CXL (January, 1973), 76

Writings about Sylvia Plath

A. Books—1960

None

B. Articles—1960

1   ALVAREZ, A. "The Poet and the Poetess." <u>London
      Observer</u> (December 18, 1960), p.12
         Although <u>The Colossus</u> has some faults, it is
    an excellent book. "The language is bare but
    vivid and precise, with a concentration that im-
    plies a good deal of disturbance with propor-
    tionately little fuss."

2   BERGONZI, BERNARD. "The Ransom Note." <u>Manchester
      Guardian</u> (November 25, 1960), p.9
         <u>The Colossus</u> is written with an assurance
    and skill rare among contemporary poets and is
    a fine first book. Mentions the influences of
    Roethke and Ransom on Plath's Work.

3   BLACKBURN, THOMAS. "Poetic Knowledge." <u>New States-
      man</u>, LX (December 24, 1960), 1016
         Praises Plath's <u>The Colossus</u> and notes the
    similarity between it and Ted Hughes' poetry.

4 DICKINSON, PETER. "Some Poets." Punch, CCIXL (De-
       cember 7, 1960), 829
           The poems in The Colossus display concrete
       experiences arranged in clean, easy verse,
       ornate where necessary." Plath expresses a
       gloomy, but exhilarating, outlook.

5 MORRAES, DOM. "Poems From Many Parts." Time and
       Tide, XLI (November, 1960), 143
           The Colossus demonstrates that Plath
       possesses great poetic skill, which far sur-
       passes her English contemporaries. Her writing
       is frequently similar to Theodore Roethke's and
       sometimes even better. Although Plath's
       ability and "zest" cause her to be too long,
       "she has learnt her craft all the way."

A. Books--1961

None

B. Articles--1961

1 DEARMER, GEOFFREY. "Sow's Ears and Silk Purses."
       Poetry Review, LII (July-September, 1961), 167
           The Colossus is "a revelation suitcase, bulg-
       ing, always accurate, humour completely un-
       forced, wresting a certain beauty from the per-
       haps too-often-preferred ugly, but with a con-
       trol and power of expression unsurpassed in
       modern poetry of the kind."

2 DYSON, A. E. "Reviews and Comments." Critical
       Quarterly, III (Summer, 1961), 181-185
           The Colossus establishes Sylvia Plath as a
       notable contemporary poet and, certainly, one of
       the best female poets seen in some time. The

DYSON, A. E. (cont.)
    encounter with nature, the devitalized humanity,
    and death are the major themes of the book.
    Plath is contrasted with Ted Hughes.

3 FULLER, ROY. "Book Reviews." London Magazine,
        VIII (March, 1961), 69-70
        The Colossus is a very well written volume,
    both in content and technique. But Plath may
    be too much in control of her verse and need a
    loosening in order to free her verse from a sort
    of over-poetized aura.

4 "Innocence and Experience," London Times Literary
        Supplement (August 18, 1961), p.550
        Reviews The Colossus. Responds to Plath's
    "vivid" and "disturbing" images. Complains
    about the "elusive and private" nature of her
    poetry, but feels it has surface clarity.

5 SARGEANT, HOWARD. "Poetry Review." English, XIII
        (Spring, 1961), 157
        In The Colossus, Sylvia Plath is "unusually
    reserved and precise." This collection is very
    well done and "what few defects there are in
    this distinguished first volume are due more to
    her sudden descents into fantasy than to any
    failure of craftsmanship."

6 WAIN, JOHN. "Farewell to the World." Spectator,
        CCVI (January 13, 1961), 50
        Sylvia Plath has quickly found an individual,
    original poetic voice. She writes very well
    and is noticeably concerned with the construc-
    tion of each line. The Colossus does demon-
    strate the influences of Stevens and Roethke.

A. Books—1962

None

B. Articles—1962

1 BURKE, HERBERT C. "Poetry." <u>Library Journal</u>,
     LXXXVII (June 15, 1962), 2385-2386
          <u>The Colossus</u> conforms to C. Day Lewis' com-
     ment on serious modern poetry: poetry "does
     things which prose could never do but also pur-
     posely avoids doing what prose could do."

2 DICKEY, WILLIAM. "Responsibilities." <u>Kenyon Re-
     view</u>, XXIV (Autumn, 1962), 760-764
          Plath's use of language in <u>The Colossus</u> dis-
     plays a careful searching for correctness; no
     word leads the reader to question its propriety.
     "Her most serious question: how are the object
     and the emotion interpenetrated, what effect has
     each on the other?"

3 HURD, PEARL STRACHAM. "Poetry." <u>Christian Science
     Monitor</u> (August 20, 1962), p.9c
          <u>The Colossus</u> is a fine first book, showing
     skill in the creation of metaphors and images.

4 KING, NICHOLAS. "Poetry: A Late Summer Roundup."
     <u>New York Herald-Tribune</u> (August 26, 1962), p.4
          Plath "shows exceptional promise" in <u>The
     Colossus</u>. She speaks in an "objective language
     that is pure, drama-less and often arresting."
     Her objectivity expresses more of an attitude
     than a conviction.

5 MYERS, E. LUCAL. "The Tranquilized Fifties."
     <u>Sewanee Review</u>, LXX (Spring, 1962), 216-217
          Reviews <u>The Colossus</u>. Finds the poems

MYERS, E. LUCAL (cont.)
"impressive for control of form and tone."
Praises Plath's ability to achieve distance from
her experiences.

6   SARGEANT, HOWARD. "Poetry Review." English, XIV
(Summer, 1962), 74
In American Poetry Now, Sylvia Plath has pro-
vided a useful introduction through her selec-
tion of poems to the work of Howard Nemerov,
Adrienne Rich, Anne Sexton, and Anthony Hecht.

7   SIMON, JOHN. "More Brass than Enduring." Hudson
Review, XV (Autumn, 1962), 464
Reviews The Colossus. Believes Plath will
convert the faults of youth into "the proper
pursuits of poetry. . . ." Time, deepening perception, and stronger control will effect this.

8   WHITMORE, REED. "The Colossus and Other Poems."
Carleton Miscellany, III (Fall, 1962), 89
Praises Plath's grasp of rhetoric and her
control and compares her to Marianne Moore.

A. Books--1963

None

B. Articles--1963

1   ALVAREZ, A. "A Poet's Epitaph." London Observer
(February 17, 1963), p.23
A tribute to Sylvia Plath written the week
of her death. In her last poems, "she was sys-
tematically probing that narrow, violent area
between the viable and the impossible, between

29

ALVAREZ, A. (cont.)
experience which can be transmuted into poetry
and that which is overwhelming." Her last work
is an innovation in contemporary poetry.

2 _____. "Sylvia Plath." The Review, 9 (October,
1963), 20-26. Reprinted in The Art of Sylvia
Plath and Beyond All This Fiddle.
In the poems in The Colossus Plath uses "her
art to keep the disturbance, out of which she
made her verse, at a distance." The poems in
this volume are highly structured and rhetorical.
But in Ariel, Plath is able to transcend her
early reticence and produce a poetry of great
intensity and profoundly relevant to her own experience. At each step, Alvarez relates the
changes in her work to a biographical event
(i.e., the birth of a child and a breakthrough
into a new poetic style). This essay is the
edited transcript of a talk on the B.B.C. Third
Programme.

3 BUTLER, ROBERT. "New American Fiction: Three Dis-
appointing Novels--But One Good One." Time and
Tide, XLIV (January 31, 1963), 34
The Bell Jar handles "the tricky theme" of
mental illness very well and honestly. "Victoria Lucas" is adept and skillful.

4 HAMILTON, IAN. "Poetry." London Magazine, III
(July, 1963), 54-56
Basically deals with The Colossus. Dis-
agrees somewhat with A. Alvarez's review in the
London Observer. Agrees that Plath has gained
in intensity and "seriousness of purpose," but
does not believe her poems are perfect or a
"'totally new breakthrough for modern verse.'"

HAMILTON, IAN (cont.)
     Praises Plath's sophistication and use of
     imagery. Feels that transmitting nightmare ex-
     perience into poetry was Plath's difficulty;
     her triumph was in sometimes achieving this.

5 HOWARD, RICHARD. "Five Poets." Poetry, CI (March,
        1963), 412-413. Reprinted in Poetry, CCXXI
        (October, 1972), 54-55
          In The Colossus, Sylvia Plath's "eye is
     sharp . . . and her wits responsive to what she
     sees. She prefers, though, to make you hear
     what she sees, the texture of her language
     affording a kind of analogue for the experience
     she presents." The last poem in the volume,
     "The Stones," appears to be a new breakthrough,
     a new voice speaking of despair.

6 HUGHES, TED. Encounter, XXI (October, 1963), 45
          Biographical note on Plath preceding ten of
     her poems.

7 JEROME, JUDSON. "A Poetry Chronicle--Part I."
        Antioch Review, XXIII (Spring, 1963), 110-111
          Reviews The Colossus. Especially admires
     Plath's response to life. Mentions imagery of
     seascapes and her allegorical approach. Finds
     her poetry an "exciting discovery."

8 LERNER, LAURENCE. "New Novels." Listener, LXIX
        (January 31, 1963), 215
          The Bell Jar triumphs in its criticism of
     American society and its language. The author
     has "an almost poetic delicacy of perception.
     This is a brilliant and moving book."

9   "Under the Skin." London Times Literary Supplement
        (January 25, 1963), p.53
            The Bell Jar is a "considerable achievement"
        for "Victoria Lucas," who writes admirably and
        with a real ability for creating new worlds for
        the reader.

10 OWEN, GUY. Books Abroad, XXXVII (Spring, 1963), 209
            Review of The Colossus. The poems show
        Plath's talent and craftsmanship. Her rhymes
        are "mint-new." Plath pushes alliteration and
        assonance to the breaking point and "there is
        seldom any straining for effect."

11 RAVEN, SIMON. "The Trouble With Phaedra." Specta-
        tor, CCX (February 15, 1963), 202-203
            Short mention of The Bell Jar as "unpleasant,
        competent and often very funny."

12 STARBUCK, GOERGE. "Sylvia Plath." Spectator, CCX
        (February 22, 1963), 220
            States the tragedy of Plath's suicide.

13 TAUBMAN, ROBERT. "Anti-heroes." New Statesman,
        LXVI (January 25, 1963), 128
            The Bell Jar is a "clever first novel" and
        the first novel by a female in the Salinger
        attitude.

A. Books--1964

None

B. Articles--1964

1   JONES, A. R. AND C. B. COX. "After the Tranquil-
        ized Fifties: Notes on Sylvia Plath and James
        Baldwin." Critical Quarterly, VI (Summer, 1964),

JONES, A. R. AND C. B. COX (cont.)
    107-122. Partially reprinted in The Art of
    Sylvia Plath.
        Extensive commentary on "Daddy," a poem
    which deals with the intimate relationship be-
    tween love and brutality and the peculiar type
    of cultural schizophrenia which it produces.
    Compares "Daddy to Lowell's "91 Revere Street"
    and Sexton's "Sylvia's Death."

A. Books--1965

None

B. Articles--1965

1 ALVAREZ, A. "Poetry in Extremis." London Observer
        (March 14, 1965), p.26
            Plath's Ariel presents poems which explore
        the extremes of her simultaneous involvement
        with and detachment from her own life. Her work
        "has an originality that keeps it apart from any
        poetic fads. It is too concentrated and de-
        tached and ironic for 'confessional' verse, with
        all that implies of self-indulgent cashing-in on
        misfortunes." In Ariel, Plath goes beyond her
        earlier stylistic and thematic concerns to a
        completely new area for contemporary poetry.

2 FURBANK, P. N. "New Poetry." Listener, LXXIII
        (March 11, 1965), 379
            "It is no good pretending that Sylvia Plath's
        is not sick verse." The poems in Ariel sacri-
        fice all of their art and spirit to Plath's
        psychological disintegration.

3 HOPE, FRANCIS. "Suffer and Observe." <u>New States-</u>
       <u>man</u>, LXIX (April 30, 1965), 687-688
          The poems in <u>Ariel</u> refuse to let the reader
       forget the circumstances of Plath's life, even
       though he should. The greatness of Plath's
       talent is obscure.

4 HORDER, JOHN. "Reviews." <u>Outposts</u>, 66 (Autumn,
       1965), 24-25
          After the first emotional impact caused by
       the poems in <u>Ariel</u> passed, it can be seen that
       Plath's reputation, which rests on about three
       poems, is really the reason for her success than
       her ability as a poet. "The bulk of <u>Ariel</u> is
       disappointing by the standards she sets her-
       self."

5 HUGHES, TED. "<u>Ariel</u>." <u>The Poetry Book Society</u>
       <u>Bulletin</u>, 44 (February, 1965), 1
          Comments on the content and background of the
       poems in <u>Ariel</u>. They create "a Paradise which
       is at the same time eerily frightening, an un-
       alterably spotlit vision of death."

6 JONES, A. R. "Necessity and Freedom: The Poetry of
       Robert Lowell, Sylvia Plath, and Anne Sexton."
       <u>Critical Quarterly</u>, VII (Spring, 1965), 11-30
          Discussion of Lowell, Plath, and Sexton as
       similar revolutionaries, although they are also,
       paradoxically, "extremely traditional poets" in
       the Romantic sense. The comments on Plath al-
       most exclusively concern <u>Ariel</u>.

7 "Poems for the Good-Hearted." <u>London Times</u> (Novem-
       ber 4, 1965), p.15b
          The poems in <u>Ariel</u> "at their best combine an
       exact and powerful delineation of cruel and self-

"Poems for the..." (cont.)
    destructive emotion with a brave wit or a deter-
    mined hanging-on to happiness. They are noble
    poems."

8   "Along the Edge." London Times Literary Supplement
        (November 25, 1965), p.1071
            The poems in Ariel present a world propelled
        by "fears, or nightmarish impulses toward bru-
        tality or suicide." Though some of the poems
        sound like parodies of a Plath poem, those that
        succeed "make this one of the most marvellous
        volumes of poetry published for a very long
        time." Comments at length on "Daddy."

9   OETTLE, PAMELA. "Sylvia Plath's Last Poems."
        Balcony, III (1965), 47-50
            Brief statements on the critical reception of
        Ariel and biographical details. The poems in
        The Colossus are "clever, literary, borrowed,"
        but those in Ariel are "assured, colloquial,
        harshly and violently her own." Comments brief-
        ly on some of the more frequently mentioned
        poems in Ariel.

10 PARKER, DEREK. "Ariel, Indeed." Poetry Review, LVI
        (Summer, 1965), 118-120
            Although when reading Ariel one cannot help
        remembering the way in which Sylvia Plath died,
        the poems are remarkable in themselves and are
        not merely considered so because of the poet's
        life.

11 PRESS, JOHN. "Two Poets." Punch, CCXLVIII (March
        31, 1965), 486
            Plath "was endowed with a rare vitality and
        intensity." The poems in Ariel express her
        dedication and demand that the reader experience
        the pain concerned in the content.

12 ROSENTHAL, M. L. "Poets of the Dangerous Way."
      Spectator, CCXIV (March 19, 1965), 367
          Combined review of Lowell's For the Union
      Dead and Ariel. Lowell is the source for
      Plath's use of the confessional mode. Her
      poems, although there are "some lovely poems,"
      stress her identification with the horrible
      aspects of the modern world.

13 ROSS, ALAN. "Selected Books." London Magazine, V
      (May, 1965), 99-101
          Reviews Ariel. Dwells on the agony of imag-
      ing "mutilation of the personality." Comments
      on color images using black, white and red--
      assigning symbolic meaning to their usage.
      Evaluates the poems as "beyond art," belonging
      rather to life, intense and clear, but finally
      more rightfully to be seen as acts of courage.

14 SKELTON, ROBIN. "Britannia's Muse Revisited."
      Massachusetts Review, VI (Autumn, 1965), 834-835
          In Ariel, Plath "has left us poetry that
      seems to me to be central to the fifties and
      sixties in which poetry of violence and 'confes-
      sional' poetry became more in evidence than ever
      before." Mentions the influence of Roethke.

15 STEINER, GEORGE. "Dying is an Art." Reporter,
      XXXIII (October 7, 1965), 51-54. Reprinted in
      Language and Silence and The Art of Sylvia
      Plath.
          Deals with the Plath legend and her great
      effect on English readers by discussing several
      of the poems in The Colossus and Ariel. Gen-
      erally, Steiner praises Plath's work--"Daddy"
      is the "'Guernica' of modern poetry"--and offers
      a number of suggestions on influences (Lawrence,
      Dickinson, Stevens, Marvell, Lowell and the

STEINER, GEORGE (cont.)
    Jacobean dramatists). He also stresses the
    gothic elements in her work, which early is
    forced and unsuccessful but later produces the
    peculiar nightmarish effect of her poetry.

A. Books—1966

None

B. Articles—1966

1 AMES, LOIS. "Notes Toward a Biography." Tri-Quar-
        terly, 7 (Fall, 1966), 95-107. Reprinted in
        The Art of Sylvia Plath.
            Biographical article on Plath. The stated
        purpose is to present the available facts on
        her life without any extensive comments on her
        work. Quotes many of Plath's written reactions
        to various events in her life.

2 BARO, GENE. "Varied Quintet." New York Times (June
        26, 1966), VI, pp.10, 12
            The public reputation of Plath coupled with
        her image as a martyred poet tends to obscure
        her work and make it seem a bit grander than it
        really is. Her primary achievement is an
        ability to create startling images. But when
        one goes beyond the glittering surfaces of the
        poems, the thought is "not always of a distin-
        guished quality." "Even within Miss Plath's
        fine skill and inventiveness, the poems some-
        times fail. Overall, their manner and feeling
        is monotonous, though their imagery is not."

3   BEWLEY, G. MARIUS. "Poetry Chronicle." Hudson Re-
      view, XIX (Autumn, 1966), 491
         Ariel does not seem to merit the critical
      praise generally accorded to it. A poem is
      founded upon its imagery, and it is hard to find
      in the images employed in Ariel "a decisively
      shaping attitude toward experience."

4   CLAIRE, WILLIAM F. "The Rare Random Descent: The
      Poetry and Pathos of Sylvia Plath." Antioch
      Review, XXVI (Winter, 1966-1967), 552-560
         Biographical article dealing with Plath as
      "a contemporary Ariel who came to reflect the
      time through unified and directly honest poems."
      Comments on the facts of Plath's life and the
      relationship between her poetry and these bio-
      graphical facts.

5   DAVISON, PETER. "Inhabited by a Cry: The Last
      Poetry of Sylvia Plath." Atlantic, CCXVIII
      (August, 1966), 76-77
         Ariel is a revelation of Plath's true genius--
      the best of her writings. These poems are the
      result of "long, deliberate, technical training"
      and possess a "ritual ring, the inevitable pre-
      face to doom."

6   DYSON, A. E. "On Sylvia Plath." Tri-Quarterly, 7
      (Fall, 1966), 75-80. Reprinted in The Art of
      Sylvia Plath.
         Recounts Dyson's introduction to Sylvia Plath
      and her work, explores some of the major ele-
      ments in her poetry, and offers some general re-
      marks on her importance. Her work faces "our
      present nuclear world fully," exceeds the "ter-
      rifying" views of Yeats, Eliot and Joyce, and
      offers some slight hope for redemption.

7   HUGHES, TED. "Notes on the Chronological Order of
       Sylvia Plath's Poems." Tri-Quarterly, 7 (Fall,
       1966), 81-88. Reprinted in The Art of Sylvia
       Plath.
          Hughes comments on the subject matter and
       chronology of the poems in The Colossus and
       Ariel, as well as makes some general statements
       ments on Plath's work as a whole.

8   JAFFE, DAN. "An All-American Muse." Saturday Re-
       view IV (October 15, 1966), 29
          Reviews Ariel. Reacts negatively to the
       "case history" tone of the poems. Feels they
       are the "dead-end of romanticism." Believes
       Ariel is a failure because of its sameness, its
       lack of surprise.

9   KENNER, HUGH. "Arts and the Age." Triumph (Septem-
       ber, 1966), 33-34
          Plath's Ariel is not the shriek of a poet go-
       ing mad, but a well contrived and constructed
       poetic statement. Kenner discusses the mythic
       image of Plath as a suicidal victim as possibly
       originating in her own "bogus spirituality" of
       the tormented soul, a position which apparently
       appeals to thousands.

10 KLEIN, ELINOR. "A Friend Recalls Sylvia Plath."
       Glamour (November, 1966), 168, 182-184
          Elinor Klein, a friend of Plath's since the
       fall of 1954, attempts to give a more human
       image to the poet. "Except for two illnesses,
       including the last which consumed her, Sylvia
       Plath was not the incarnation of the mad, ob-
       sessed poetess. Sylvia was a golden girl who
       knew more about living then most." Biographical
       detail on Plath is provided for the period 1954
       to 1963.

11 LASK, THOMAS. "Books of the Times: A Kind of Hero-
        ism." New York Times (June 8, 1966), p.45
        The poems in Ariel deal with the closest
    human relationships in an intense exploration of
    the self. Her writing displays "a nervous
    energy almost as if the ideas came into her con-
    sciousness in staccato fashion." She is also
    skilled in the use of rhyme (particularly in
    "Daddy") and expression.

12 LOWELL, ROBERT. "Foreward" in Ariel. New York:
        Harper and Row, 1966, vii-ix
        The poems in Ariel show Plath becoming "one
    of those super-real, hypnotic, great classical
    heroines." They invert the conventional idea of
    the feminine into a totally new concept and deal
    with life in such a way as to tell that it "is
    simply not worth it." "Probably many, after
    reading Ariel, will recoil from their first
    overawed shock, and painfully wonder why so much
    of it leaves them feeling empty, evasive and in-
    articulate."

13 MADDOCKS, MELVIN. "Sylvia Plath: The Cult and the
        Poems." Christian Science Monitor (June 30,
        1966), p.11
        Ariel is a remarkable book, but not so re-
    markable as the Plath cultists would have one
    believe. "It is a frantically one-sided nay-
    saying, written at the breaking point with all
    defenses down."

14 NEWMAN, CHARLES. "Candor is the Only Wile: The Art
        of Sylvia Plath." Tri-Quarterly, 7 (Fall,
        1966), 39-64. Reprinted in The Art of Sylvia
        Plath.
        An exploration of Plath's work in terms of
    her artistic stance, poetic tradition, themes,

NEWMAN, CHARLES (cont.)
Romanticism, and her evolution "in poetic voice
from the precocious girl, to the disturbed
modern woman, to the vengeful magician, to—
Ariel—God's lioness." Compares Plath to Emily
Dickinson throughout.

15 ORR, PETER. The Poet Speaks. London: Routledge and
Kegan Paul, 1966, 167-172
Interview with Plath which took place on
October 30, 1962. Plath discusses her background, influences on her poetry, her interest
in fiction and the type of people she feels most
comfortable with.

16 ROSENTHAL, M. L. "Poetic Theory of Some Contemporary Poets." Salmagundi, I (1966-1967), 70-77
In Sylvia Plath's comments on her poetry
there is an active effort to show how the elements of the poems balance each other. "In no
instance—and the same is true of Lowell—does
the poet confine the account of a poem to the
interpretation of a purely subjective state."

17 SARGEANT, HOWARD. "Poetry Review." English, XVI
(Spring, 1966), 31
It is difficult to treat the poems in Ariel
"as other than cries of desperation." Perhaps
her death was inevitable because of her artis-
tic attitude, but it is certainly a great loss.

18 SEXTON, ANNE. "The Barfly Ought to Sing." Tri-
Quarterly, 7 (Fall, 1966)
Biographical sketch of Sexton's relationship
with Plath and George Starbuck, primarily cen-
tering on the time when they attended Robert
Lowell's class at Boston University. Includes
Sexton's poems "Wanting to Die" and "Sylvia's
Death."

19 SMITH, WILLIAM J. "New Books of Poems." Harper's
        CCXXXIII (August, 1966), 92
            Reviews Ariel. Believes the poems are filled
        with "airiness," "exhilaration," and "transcen-
        dent terror." Considers Plath's stance as
        "feminine rather than female." Mentions the
        "core" of the book to be the poems on bee-keep-
        ing; these are autobiographical and "strangely
        . . . ritual." Criticizes repetition and di-
        gressions from plot, but praises Plath's
        language.

20 STEINER, GEORGE. "Russian Roulette." Newsweek,
        LXVII (June 20, 1966), 109a-110
            Dwells on the shock effect of Ariel. Plath's
        fame will be illuminated by her "immolation."
        In her work, the major paradox is that "death
        and dissolution" convince the reader of "life."
        Plath's lyricism provides her readers with an
        "amplified sense of their humanity."

21 TAUBMAN, ROBERT. "Uncle's War." New Statesman,
        LXXII (September 16, 1966), 402
            The Bell Jar is ingenious, but unconvincing
        as a portrayal of mental breakdown and suffers
        in the comparison with her poetry.

22 "The Blood Jet Is Poetry." Time, LXXXVIII (June 10,
        1966), 118-120
            Provides the basic biographical details of
        Plath's life, comments on the intensity and
        violence of the poems in Ariel, and reprints
        "Daddy."

23 "Notes on Current Books." Virginia Quarterly Review,
        XLII (Autumn, 1966), cxl
            The poems in Ariel are "intense and frighten-
        ing." The heart is laid bare. The world

"Notes on Current..." (cont.)
    becomes the poet's enemy--"attempting to divert
    her from final commitment." The poems are
    "self-defeating without being self-indulgent."

A. Books--1967

None

B. Articles--1967

1 ALVAREZ, A. "Beyond All This Fiddle." London Times
       Literary Supplement (March 23, 1967), p.229-232
           Plath's poetry is an "extension of Lowell's
       exploration: she simply went further in the di-
       rection he had already taken."

2 BRINNIN, JOHN M. "Plath, Jarrell, Kinnell, Smith."
       Partisan Review, XXXIV (Winter, 1967), 156
           Sylvia Plath's poetry presents a rare vision
       of anguish. Anguish is not a consequence in
       her work as it is for Emily Dickinson, but "the
       whole relentless subject itself." However,
       Plath's major problem is that she overdoes her
       theme; after eighty-five pages of a shriek of
       anguish, it becomes a "bore."

3 DAVIS, DOUGLAS M. "In the Flow of Poetry, the
       Ladies Flourish." National Observer (February
       6, 1967), p.31
           Ariel is one of the best volumes of the
       decade. The subject matter of the poems is
       "uniformly domestic" and expresses a tragic
       sense of life.

4 DICKEY, JAMES. Spinning the Crystal Ball: Some
   Guesses at the Future of American Poetry. Washington, D.C.: Library of Congress, 1967, 3-4.
   Reprinted in Sorties.
        The motive behind the work of Plath, Sexton,
   and Snodgrass is "essentially therapeutic."
   "The main feeling that one has--or at least
   that I have--is of an attempt to be clever; and
   if there is one thing that I find intolerable
   in either literature or in the world, it is
   slick, knowing patter about suffering and guilt,
   particularly about one's own." The confessional
   style "is near the end of its tenure."

5 DRAKE, BARBARA. "Perfection is Terrible; It Cannot
   Have Children." Northwest Review, IX (Summer,
   1967), 101-103
        The poems in Ariel arise from Plath's percep-
   tion of imperfections in modern existence. The
   madness that seems to exist in this volume is
   produced by a view of life which looks closely
   and in detail and, at times, this is no more
   confessional than, for instance, Gulliver's
   Travels.

6 HAYMAN, RONALD. "Personal Poetry." Encounter, XXIX
   (December, 1967), 86-87
        In The Colossus, one can see the roots of
   Ariel's images and themes that eventually grew
   into her later verse and The Bell Jar.

7 HOWES, BARBARA. "A Note on Ariel." Massachusetts
   Review, VIII (Winter, 1967), 225-226
        The poems in Ariel almost demand that the
   reader become involved with the Plath biography:
   "there is so intrusive a note of self-pity and
   exhibitionism; she appears to have been a considerable solipsist, with relatively few relationships with the living."

8   "Chained to the Parish Pump." London Times Literary
        Supplement (March 16, 1967), p.220
            The Colossus displays Plath's early sophisti-
        cation and "rich image-creating energy." These
        poems show the influence of Ransom and Roethke.

9   PRESS, JOHN. "Four Poets." Punch, CCLII (April 5,
        1967), 508
            Reading The Colossus four years after Sylvia
        Plath's death, "we may detect in it traces of
        the mental pain and of the obsessions which
        later overwhelmed her." But poems concerned
        with the joy of living are much more in evidence.

10 ROSENTHAL, M. L. "Metamorphosis of a Book." Spec-
        tator, CCXVIII (April 21, 1967), 456-457
            Mentions Ariel, The Colossus, The Bell Jar.
        Concentrates on Plath's "concrete" vision in
        The Colossus. Points to images of "cold
        terror" and dead animals as haunting, and the
        theme of suicide as "pervasive." Contrariwise,
        some poems indicate a happier side, but her
        poems more characteristically show Plath's "ab-
        solute alienation from town and landscape."

11 _____. The New Poets: American and British Poetry
        Since World War II. New York: Oxford University
        Press, 1967, 79-89. Reprinted in The Art of
        Sylvia Plath.
            Plath made the ultimate identification of her
        life with her art. Her early poems were "seldom
        exciting" and restrained, but in her late work,
        where the identification becomes more acute,
        Plath comes to a violent commitment. "The evo-
        lution of her muse is one sign of the growth and
        clarification, within a brief span of months, of
        Sylvia Plath's peculiar awareness of the burden

45

B11   ABOUT SYLVIA PLATH (1967)

_____. (cont.)
of her life in the whole context of modern existence." Remarks on some of the posthumous pub-
lishing aspects of her work.

12 STEINER, GEORGE. Language and Silence. London:
Faber and Faber, 1967
Reprints "Dying Is an Art" from the Reporter.

13 SYMONS, JULIAN. "The Old Enemies." New Statesman,
LXXIII (April 7, 1967), 479
Remarks on the unique nature of Plath's
poetry. The Colossus gives no hint of the poet
that would emerge in Ariel.

14 TAYLOR, ELINOR ROSS. "Sylvia Plath's Last Poems."
Poetry, LXXIX (January, 1967), 260-262
The poems in Ariel constantly recall the
reader to the tragic facts of Plath's life. They
express an extreme of energy and impatience and
"are self-consciously womanly, yet there is a
curious underlying rejection of being a woman."
They do tend to fail, though, in their confessional quality, a quality which does not allow
the reader to feel he has "come upon a silence,
a privacy, upon intellect existing unselfcon-
sciously."

A. Books--1968

None

B. Articles--1968

1 CLEVERDON, DOUGLAS. "Introduction" in Three Women.
London: Turret Press, 1968
Discusses the background of Three Women, its
themes, and Plath's experience in broadcasting.

2 ETHRIDGE, JAMES E., BARBARA KOPALA AND CAROLYN
     RILEY, EDS. Contemporary Authors: A Bio-bibli-
     ographical Guide to Current Authors and Their
     Works. Vols. XIX-XX. Detroit: Gale, 1968,
     342-344
        Biographical details of Plath's life; pub-
     lishing history; a selection of critical com-
     ments; and a brief bibliography of works and
     locations of works.

3 HOLBROOK, DAVID. "The 200-inch Distorting Mirror."
     New Society, (July 11, 1968), 57-58
        Sylvia Plath is "a clear example of the
     schizoid writer. She expresses throughout her
     work that feeling of a hollow core at the center
     of identity--a fundamental weakness at the heart
     of being." Her work is a mixture of insanity
     and insight. Mentions the importance of R. D.
     Laing's and Leslie H. Farber's psychological
     theories in recognizing Plath's schizophrenia.

4 _____. "R. D. Laing and the Death Circuit."
     Encounter, (August, 1968), 35-45
        A brief discussion of Plath and Dylan Thomas.
     The primary focus is on the importance of R. D.
     Laing's psychological theories dealing with mad-
     ness. The Bell Jar and The Colossus are briefly
     mentioned. Plath may have sought rebirth
     through suicide.

5 HOYLE, JAMES F. "Sylvia Plath: A Poetry of Suicidal
     Mania." Literature and Psychology, XVIII (1968),
     187-203
        At times excessively psychological, this ar-
     ticle draws distinct parallels between Plath's
     "manic depression" and her poetry, especially in
     Ariel. "Sylvia Plath is an important poet for
     several reasons. One is the coherence of her
     work, what might be called the honesty of her

HOYLE, JAMES F. (cont.)
suicide. She achieves a dead end to much that
will seem ill-thought and half-hearted in even
the best modern poetry. . . . Plath will be
permanently important because her achievement
is so ironically Wordsworthian; like Freud's
achievement, it is thoroughly rooted in the
family and its problems."

6 KISSICK, GARY. "Plath: A Terrible Perfection."
Nation, CCVII (September 16, 1968), 245-247
Through a transfiguration of common images in
The Colossus and Ariel, Plath "indicts" the emp-
tiness of the modern world. Her world is a
mechanism set in motion to create and destroy
man with a "terrible perfection."

7 "Cache of Verse." London Times (December 27, 1968),
p.8g
A Collection of twenty-two unpublished poems
in Plath's manuscript "Two Lovers and a Beachcomber," which she submitted for part two of the
English tripos in the Easter term, 1957, have
been found in the English faculty library at
Cambridge. Eric Homberger commented that these
poems "suggest her style was more fully formed
and less derivative than has previously been
thought."

8 MORSE, S. F. "Poetry 1966." Contemporary Literature, IX (Winter, 1968), 127
The poems in Ariel present a painful experience, which symbolizes a great loss. Ariel is
one of the foremost volumes of poetry in 1966,
"for it is, of its kind, an absolute achievement."

9   OBERG, ARTHUR K. "Sylvia Plath and the New Deca-
       dence." Chicago Review, XX (1968), 66-73
         "Sylvia Plath's work is less a collection of
       poems than a distinctive decor that is related
       to a new decadence in art." Plath made the ul-
       timate confusion of life and art, and her poems
       tend to reflect this in the easy biographical
       application. Stasis, perfection, and death are
       her major themes.

10   OSTRIKER, ALICIA. "'Fact' as Style: The Americani-
       zation of Sylvia." Language and Style, I (Sum-
       mer, 1968), 201-212
         The change in Plath's work from The Colossus
       to Ariel arises from a desire to express a
       clearer picture of reality. The Colossus is the
       "safer" work, more traditional and less intro-
       spective than Ariel. Plath's use of language
       and her disregard of poetic convention in the
       search for reality is comparable to the whole
       tradition of American literature. "The method
       is a kind of journalism of obsessions--hasty,
       flashy, but it works."

11   STILWELL, ROBERT. "The Multiplying Entities: D. H.
       Lawrence and Five Other Poets." Sewanee Review,
       LXXVI (Summer, 1968), 530-533
         The poems in Ariel should be judged on their
       own merit and not exclusively as autobiographi-
       cal documents from a tragic life. In the main,
       the poems are not about the subject of psychosis,
       but poems "which find their fullest analogies in
       the visions and emotional states and awful in-
       sights of psychosis." The poems are repetitious.
       Ariel will not "add a major dimension to the
       poetry of the 1960's."

A   ABOUT SYLVIA PLATH (1969)

A. Books—1969

None

B. Articles—1969

1 ALVAREZ, A. <u>Beyond All This Fiddle</u>. New York:
      Random House, 1969
         Reprints "Beyond All This Fiddle" from the
      <u>London Times Literary Supplement</u> (3-21) and
      "Sylvia Plath" from <u>The Review</u> (45-58).

2 _____. "Sylvia Plath: The Cambridge Collection."
      <u>Cambridge Review</u> (February 7, 1969).* Re-
      printed in <u>The Cambridge Mind</u>.
         Comments on Plath's manuscript submitted at
      Cambridge for the second part of the English
      tripos. In these poems, she was doing appren-
      tice work in highly formal and diverse methods
      of poetic technique.

3 BAGG, ROBERT. "The Rise of Lady Lazarus." <u>Mosaic</u>,
      II (1969), 9-36
         A discussion of "the context in which some
      exceptional modern poets discovered the self's
      various uses and its vulnerability." Yeats,
      Eliot and Lowell are those who saw a necessity
      for the self's acknowledgement of some metaphysi-
      cal structure. Plath goes beyond this and sees
      no limitations on the self. "Instead of resist-
      ing the self's antagonists she derives a tre-
      mendous thrill from throwing her imagination
      into the act of self-obliteration."

4 BOYERS, ROBERT. "Sylvia Plath: The Trepanned Veter-
      an." <u>Centennial Review</u>, XIII (Spring, 1969),
      138-153
         Plath's poetry "is generated at the expense
      of life, as the rigors of selection overwhelm

BOYERS, ROBERT (cont.)
the comforts of a more benign pluralism. The
poet selects in such a way that the diverse aspects of her experience are fixed into immu-
table categories. Locked within these relatively static structures they participate in mythic
interaction with elements of a different order,
an order deriving from broader cultural perspectives, which function similarly as categories
holding their peculiar elements in recurrent
patterns." Detailed discussion of "Daddy" and
"Cut" and remarks on the relationship between
Plath and Kafka.

5 CAMPBELL, WENDY. "Remembering Sylvia." Cambridge
Review (1969).* Reprinted in The Art of Sylvia
Plath.
Concerns Sylvia Plath's life at Cambridge,
her early life with Ted Hughes, and Campbell's
reaction to Plath's death.

6 HOWARD, RICHARD. Alone With America. New York:
Atheneum, 1969, 413-422
The Colossus is properly characterized as
Plath's "jevenilia." In this book, she explores a number of contradictory impulses, in-
coherencies that long for resolution. The
resolution is met in Ariel, where she became
"totally Other, so that she (or the poems--it is
all one now) looked back upon 'herself' as not
yet having become anything at all." Howard
relies on the use of extensive quotations from
Plath's poetry for exemplification.

7 MILLS, RALPH J. Creations Very Self: On the Personal Element in Recent American Poetry. Fort
Worth: Texas Christian University Press, 1969,
32-36
Plath's psychological state tended to free

MILLS, RALPH J. (cont.)
her from conventional stylistic traits and "per-
mit her entry into the most extreme conditions
of awareness and feeling." Her own emotional
crises serve as a universalizing agent through
which she can imaginatively experience life out-
side of herself.

8   STEINER, GEORGE. "In Extremis." Cambridge Review
(February 7, 1969).* Reprinted in The Cambridge
Mind.
        Comments on Ariel and Plath's Cambridge manu-
script. The extreme nature of her late poems
leaves Steiner "uneasy." "Does any writer, does
any human being other than an actual survivor,
have the right to put on this death-rig?" Her
work shows the influences of Hughes, Ransom,
Stevens, and Empson.

9   TILLINGHAST, RICHARD. "Worlds of Their Own."
Southern Review, V (April, 1969), 582-583
        Reviews Ariel. Feels these are poems of
schizophrenia, art of the type produced by
Bosch, Goya, and others. They are related to
the current "poetry of breakdown." Believes
Plath's madness, however, was a "means to writing great poetry."

10 ZOLLMAN, SOL. "Sylvia Plath and Imperialist Culture.
Literature and Ideology, II (1969), 11-22
        Sylvia Plath's poetry and her novel The Bell
Jar are examples of the effect of the American
"imperialist" culture on a sensitive, educated
individual. "What she goes through illustrates
the tragic consequences of a middle class intellectual career in imperialist society and the
hollowness of the bourgeois myth that the pursuit of self-interest through education is a

ZOLLMAN, SOL (cont.)
    meaningful ambition and that one's success is a
    testimony to one's moral and intellectual quali-
    ties." Plath's experience in this encounter is
    seen to be the "source of her poetry."

A. Books--1970

1 HOMBERGER, ERIC. A Chronological Checklist of the
       Periodical Publications of Sylvia Plath. Exe-
       ter: University of Exeter, 1970
           A checklist of Plath's periodical contribu-
       tions (poetry, fiction, and non-fiction)
       arranged in chronological order. This is a re-
       vision of the bibliography of Plath's works by
       Mary Kinzie in The Art of Sylvia Plath.

2 NEWMAN, CHARLES, Ed. The Art of Sylvia Plath: A
       Symposium. London: Faber and Faber, 1970. Con-
       tents: Charles Newman's "Candor Is the Only
       Wile--The Art of Sylvia Plath" (21-55). A. Al-
       varez's "Sylvia Plath" (56-68). M. L. Rosen-
       thal's "Sylvia Plath and Confessional Poetry"
       (69-76). Richard Howard's "Sylvia Plath: 'And I
       Have No Face, I Have Wanted to Efface Myself
       . . .'" (77-88). Edward Lucie-Smith's "Sea-
       imagery in the Work of Sylvia Plath" (91-99).
       Annette Lavers' "The World as Icon: On Sylvia
       Plath's Themes" (100-135). John Frederick Nims'
       "The Poetry of Sylvia Plath: A Technical Analy-
       sis" (136-152). Lois Ames' "Notes Toward A Bi-
       ography" (155-173). Anne Sexton's "The Barfly
       Ought to Sing" (174-181). Wendy Campbell's "Re-
       membering Sylvia" (182-186). Ted Hughes' "The
       Chronological Order of Sylvia Plath's Poems"
       (187-195). Stephen Spender's "Warnings From the
       Grave" (199-203). A. E. Dyson's "On Sylvia
       Plath" (204-210). George Steiner's "Dying is an

NEWMAN, CHARLES, Ed. (cont.)
    Art" (211-218). Mary Ellmann's "The Bell Jar:
An American Girlhood" (221-226). Douglas Clev-
erdon's "On Three Women" (227-229). A. R.
Jones' "On 'Daddy'" (230-236). Mary Kinzie's
"An Informal Check List of Criticism" (283-304).
Mary Kinzie, Daniel Lynn and Suzanne D. Kurman
"Bibliography" (305-319). The following works
by Sylvia Plath: "Dialogue en Route" (239-240).
"Miss Drake Proceeds to Supper" (241). "On the
Plethora of Dryads" (242-243). "Epitaph for
Fire and Flower" (244-245). "Battle-Scene From
the Comic Operatic Fantasy 'The Seafarer'" (246-
247). "Words For a Nursery" (248-249). "Mush-
rooms" (250-251). "In Plaster" (252-253). "An
Appearance" (254). "Lesbos" (255-257). "Pur-
dah" (258-259). "Mystic" (260). "Excerpt From
the Radio Play: 'Three Women'" (261-265).
"Ocean 1212-W" (266-272). "Thalidomide"
("Seven pages of poem from first handwritten
draft to final typed version.") (273-279).
Three Pen Drawings: "Wuthering Heights" (280),
"Benidorn" (281), and "Rock Harbor, Cape Cod"
(282).

B. Articles--1970

1 ELLMANN, MARY. "The Bell Jar: An American Girlhood"
    in The Art of Sylvia Plath. Ed. Charles Newman.
    London: Faber and Faber, 1970, 221-226
      Discusses the major themes of the novel
    (which possess the same "extremes" as the poems'
    content) and considers its sociological refer-
    ence to society in the United States during the
    1950's.

2 GORDON, JAN B. "'Who Is Sylvia?' The Art of Sylvia
     Plath." Modern Poetry Studies, I (1970), 6-34
       Explores Plath's poetry as documents of
     schizophrenia. Plath's art, the expression of
     her private mythology, is ultimately confused
     with her life. So, she lives and dies accord-
     ing to or because of her personal myth, which
     was the product of an ill-defined sense of self.
     Also, by reading Plath's work, the reader par-
     ticipates--experiences--"'schizoid-ness.'"

3 HARDY, BARBARA. "The Poetry of Sylvia Plath" in
     The Survival of Poetry. Ed. Martin Dodsworth.
     London: Faber and Faber, 1970, 164-187
       Briefly mentions The Colossus, but dwells on
     Ariel. Disagrees with David Holbrook's conten-
     tion (in "The 200-inch Distorting Mirror") that
     Plath wrote schizophrenic poetry that "'involves
     us in false solutions and even the huis clos
     circuits of death. . . .'" Contrariwise, Miss
     Hardy believes Plath's poems attain value
     through "imaginative enlargement" rather than
     derangement. Miss Hardy closely analyses "Nick
     and the Candlestick" and "The Swarm" from Ariel.

4 HOMBERGER, ERIC, WILLIAM JANEWAY AND SIMON SCHAMA,
     EDS. The Cambridge Mind. Boston: Little,
     Brown, 1970
       Reprints the following from The Cambridge
     Review: Plath's poems "Street Song" (296-297)
     and "Aerialist" (298-299); A. Alvarez's "Sylvia
     Plath: The Cambridge Collection" (299-303); and
     George Steiner's "In Extremis" (303-307).

5 KINZIE, MARY. "An Informal Check List of Criticism"
     in The Art of Sylvia Plath. Ed. Charles Newman.
     London: Faber and Faber, 1970, 283-304
       Partially annotated bibliography of criticism
     on Sylvia Plath arranged in chronological order.

KINZIE, MARY (cont.)
The intended purpose is "to trace the develop-
ment of the so-called 'cult' through the reviews, noting the effect her death had on the
tenor and substance of the critical comment."

6 KINZIE, MARY, DANIEL LYNN CONRAD AND SUZANNE D. KUR-
MAN. "Bibliography" in The Art of Sylvia Plath.
Ed. Charles Newman. London: Faber and Faber,
1970, 305-319
A bibliography of Sylvia Plath's works
arranged by type and alphabetically.

7 LAVERS, ANNETTE. "The World as Icon: On Sylvia
Plath's Themes" in The Art of Sylvia Plath. Ed.
Charles Newman. London: Faber and Faber, 1970,
100-135
By a formal categorization of the images in
Plath's poetry, Lavers "discovers" the icono-
graphical themes that are reflected throughout.
The poems "derive their meaning, both profound
and sometimes literal, from an underlying code,
in which objects and their qualities are endowed
with stable significations, and hierarchized."

8 LUCIE-SMITH, EDWARD. "Sea-Imagery in the Work of
Sylvia Plath" in The Art of Sylvia Plath. Ed.
Charles Newman. London: Faber and Faber, 1970,
91-99
The myth surrounding Sylvia Plath has tended
to develop the notion that there is an extreme,
drastic division in her work between the publi-
cations of The Colossus and Ariel. Although a
change is present, "I believe this view of her
work is a false one, and that she really was a
writer of exceptional and persistent unity."
This unity is illustrated by Plath's use of sea-
imagery in The Colossus, The Bell Jar, Ariel,
and Uncollected Poems.

9 NIMS, JOHN FREDERICK. "The Poetry of Sylvia Plath:
   A Technical Analysis" in The Art of Sylvia
   Plath. Ed. Charles Newman. London: Faber and
   Faber, 1970, 136-152
      A discussion of Sylvia Plath's poetics in
   The Colossus and Ariel. Plath is particularly
   adept in her use of metaphor.

10 PERLOFF, MARJORIE. "Angst and Animism in the
   Poetry of Sylvia Plath." Journal of Modern Literature, I (1970), 57-74
      A chronological discussion of Plath's poetry.
   There is a definite attempt to avoid a strict
   biographical reading of her work and stress the
   "oracular" content. Plath is viewed as being
   within the tradition of the late eighteenth century poets Blake and Collins, a relationship
   which is developed by Perloff's use of Northrop
   Frye's approach to this tradition.

11 SALAMON, LYNDA B. "'Double, Double': Perception in
   the Poetry of Sylvia Plath." Spirit, XXXVIII
   (1970), 34-39
      Central to Plath's poetry is the "contrast
   between real terror and apparent safety." This
   "double vision" produces the peculiar horror
   frequently noticed in her work and is also the
   root of Robert Lowell's comment that Plath's
   poetry is a "controlled hallucination."

12 SPEARS, MONROE K. Dionysus and the City. New York:
   Oxford University Press, 1970, 239, 247, 263
      Briefly mentions Plath as being influenced
   by Lowell. Plath's Ariel and Anne Sexton's To
   Bedlam and Part Way Back are the "full flowering" of the experimental confessional mode.

13 SUMNER, NAN MC GOWAN. "Sylvia Plath." Research
      Studies of Washington State University, XXXVIII
      (June, 1970), 112-121
          General article on Plath's poetry with atten-
      tion to the autobiographical nature of her work
      and the work itself in critical appraisal.

14 WILLIAMSON, ALAN. "The Future of Confession."
      Shenandoah, XXI (Summer, 1970), 89
          The confessional style of poetry can fre-
      quently degenerate to the idea of a mechanical
      prescription in which certain methods of self-
      expression will inevitably yield a profound
      poem. Though recognizing the possibilities of
      Lowell's stylistic methods, Plath never followed
      them "except as an abstract ideal; stylistical-
      ly, she virtually reinvented the very idea of
      'confession' from scratch."

A. Books--1971

None

B. Articles--1971

1 ADAMS, PHOEBE. "Short Reviews: Books." Atlantic,
     CCXXVII (May, 1971), 114
         The Bell Jar, although a promising first
     novel, is really not very good. The implication
     is that Plath only wrote the novel because she
     received a grant to produce it.

2 AIRD, EILEEN. "Reviews and Comment." Critical
     Quarterly, XII (Autumn, 1971), 286-288
         Crossing the Water, which contains poems
     written between those in The Colossus and Ariel,
     demonstrates the unity of Plath's work. Many of

AIRD, EILEEN (cont.)
    the poems are not fully successful, several have
    obvious biographical parallels, and some are
    masterful. The book "is undoubtedly a valuable
    and welcome addition to the body of Sylvia
    Plath's works."

3   _____. "Sylvia Plath: A Memoir." Intellectual Di-
        gest, II (November, 1971), 90-95
            Reprints Alvarez's essay from The New Ameri-
        can Review.

4   ALVAREZ, A. "Publish and Be Damned." London Ob-
        server (October 1, 1971), p.36
            The publication of Crossing the Water and
        Winter Trees raises doubts about the editorial
        motivation behind these books: both volumes to-
        gether comprise only about one-hundred pages and
        some poems written in the same periods have been
        mysteriously left out. What is needed, to pre-
        serve Plath's artistic integrity, is a collected
        edition of her works, including all of the ma-
        terial that must still remain in manuscript as
        well as that in the public domain. Several rea-
        sons for the present manner of publication might
        be involved: Plath's popularity, her image as
        the suffering woman, the economic potentiality
        of her work, and the possible intimate nature of
        her unpublished work.

5   _____. "Sylvia Plath: The Road to Suicide." London
        Observer (November 14, 1971), p.25
            An excerpt from The Savage God.

6   _____. London Observer (November 21, 1971), p.10
            Reply to Ted Hughes' letter to the editor of
        the Observer, which immediately precedes. Al-
        varez defends his right to publish his memoir on
        Plath. There was no need to consult Hughes, but

_____. (cont.)
as far as accuracy is concerned Olwyn Hughes
(Ted Hughes' sister and Plath's agent) contacted
Alvarez after the American periodical publication of the memoir and corrected two rather
small discrepancies, which are described.

7 _____. "Sylvia Plath: A Memoir" in The New American
Review. New York: Simon and Schuster, 1971, 9-
40.
Alvarez's comments and recollections on Sylvia Plath's personality, poetry and, briefly,
marriage to Ted Hughes. Especially important
is his discussion of Plath's final days, just
before her suicide. This essay also appears in
London Observer, Intellectual Digest, and The
Savage God.

8 _____. The Savage God. London: Weidenfield and
Nicholson, 1971. New York: Random House, 1972,
5-34
Includes Alvarez's "Sylvia Plath: A Memoir."

9 AMES, LOIS. "Sylvia Plath: A Biographical Note" in
The Bell Jar. New York: Harper and Row, 1971
A biographical essay on Plath, which has the
obvious force of causing readers of The Bell
Jar in this edition to look upon it as a dis-
tinctly autobiographical novel.

10 "Reservations." Antioch Review, XXXI (Winter, 1971-
1972), 587
Crossing the Water contains Plath's most ma-
ture, intensely controlled, and skillful poems.
The last poems are quite obviously moving
towards Ariel.

11 BIERMAN, LARRY. "The Vivid Tulips Eat My Oxygen:
     An Essay on Sylvia Plath's Ariel." Windless
     Orchids, IV (February, 1971), 44-46
          Ariel is Plath's demonstration of a need for
     suicide, a need accomplished through her work.
     It is evident throughout this volume that the
     author "delights in the smallest part of death."

12 BIRSTEIN, ANN. "The Sylvia Plath Cult." Vogue,
     CLVIII (October 1, 1971), 176
          Sylvia Plath has become a mythic heroine of
     the feminist movement. She "is no heroine for
     this or any other movement. Because, alas, that
     girl was dead from the beginning, passionately,
     madly in love with death." Birstein speaks of
     the cheerful Sylvia Plath she knew at Smith.
     The Bell Jar is full of self-pity; Ariel is "a
     magnificent burst of poems."

13 BLODGETT, E. D. "Sylvia Plath: Another View."
     Modern Poetry Studies, II (1971), 97-106
          The cult now surrounding Sylvia Plath does
     not grow from a response to her poetry, but to
     the poet as a sufferer, a modern. The object
     of Plath's work is to find stasis and uniform-
     ity; it refuses movement and seeks to avoid
     risk. Plath's "besetting flaw seems to have
     been that she took herself more seriously than
     her art."

14 BROWNJOHN, ALAN. "Awesome Fragments." New States-
     man, LXXXII (October 1, 1971), 446-448
          Almost all of the poems in Winter Trees "have
     the familiar Plath daring, the same feel of bits
     of frightened, vibrant, indignant consciousness
     translated instantly into words and images that

BROWNJOHN, ALAN (cont.)
blend close, experienced horror and icy, sar-
donic control." Plath is able to write certain
poems that exist only for themselves and are un-
related to experience.

15 DAVENPORT, GUY. "Novels in Braille." National Review, XXIII (May 18, 1971), 538
Sylvia Plath's The Bell Jar displays several
weaknesses, "all sins of the amateur." The
book might be interesting to Plath's coterie.

16 DICKEY, JAMES. Sorties. Garden City: Doubleday,
1971, 190-192
Reprints Dickey's Spinning the Crystal Ball.

17 DUFFY, MARTHA. "Lady Lazarus." Time, XCVII (June
21, 1971), 87-88
Comments on the background of The Bell Jar,
biographical details of Plath's life, and the
plot of the novel.

18 _____. "The Triumph of a Tormented Poet." Life,
LXXI (November 12, 1971), 38a-38b
Close reading of The Bell Jar as conforming
to the details of Plath's life. This article
stresses the wide response to Plath's work and
personality as evidence of the tortured poet,
especially her great popularity and appeal with
youth and the Women's Liberation movement. Illustrated.

19 DUNN, DOUGLAS. "Damaged Instruments." Encounter,
(August, 1971), 68-70
Although the poems in The Colossus are
"flawed by a rhymical and lexical vulgarity,"
they are unmistakably by the author of Ariel.
Crossing the Water is much freer in style than
The Colossus, and the imagery begins to have

DUNN, DOUGLAS (cont.)
some of the characteristic elements found in
Ariel. Crossing the Water contains "sustained
poems of great quality." The innovative char-
acter of these poems is "an improved sense of
drama, much stronger narrative interest," and a
stylistic change in Plath's approach.

20 FRADOS, JULIA ALDRICH. "Letters." New York Times
(June 20, 1971), VII, p.34
The romanticizing of Sylvia Plath's death
"into some kind of literary event" tends to blur
the real tragedy of her life.

21 HARDWICK, ELIZABETH. "On Sylvia Plath." New York
Review of Books, XII (August 12, 1971), 3-4, 6
Comments on the progress of Sylvia Plath
through The Bell Jar, Crossing the Water, and
Ariel. The concern is less with Plath's poetics
than it is with her personality as a poet. Us-
ing extensive biographical material, Hardwick
protrays Plath as a suffering and sensitive, but
also remarkably bold and self-confident individual.

22 HILL, WILLIAM B. "Fiction." America, CXXV (November 20, 1971), 432
Plot synopsis of The Bell Jar. Plath's
unique talent is depicted in this autobiographical novel.

23 HOWES, VICTOR. "'I am silver and exact.'" Christian Science Monitor (September 20, 1971), p.8
"Crossing the Water's transitional nature
should not be allowed to obscure its genuine
merit." This book reveals Plath's growing dra-
matic ability. Plath is superb in her descrip-
tions of "sharply observed images."

24 HUGHES, TED. "Sylvia Plath's Crossing the Water:
       Some Reflections." Critical Quarterly, XIII
       (Summer, 1971), 165–171
          Hughes discusses the background to the poems
       in Crossing the Water and gives specific commen-
       tary on nine poems which are reprinted
       ("Candles," "Sleep in the Mojave Desert,"
       "Crossing the Water," "Wuthering Heights," "In-
       somniac," "Mirror," "In Plaster," "Last Words,"
       and "An Appearance").

25 _____. "Sylvia Plath." London Observer (November
       21, 1971), p.10
          Letter to the editor in which Hughes says
       that he had no knowledge of A. Alvarez's memoir
       of Sylvia Plath. If he had, he "would have made
       more effort to see it and check the nature and
       accuracy of his facts." Alvarez's reply di-
       rectly follows.

26 KAMEEN, PAUL. Best Sellers, XXXI (November 1, 1971),
       347–348
          Crossing the Water provides the necessary in-
       formation so that the transition in Plath's work
       from The Colossus to Ariel can be seen. "The
       technical, thematic, and imaginative wealth of
       Crossing the Water proves that her poetry can
       stand unattended by her legend." Briefly com-
       ments on the subject-object conflict in her
       work.

27 LEHMANN-HAUPT, CHRISTOPHER. "An American Edition--
       At Last." New York Times (April 16, 1971), p.35
          Briefly discusses the background and plot of
       The Bell Jar. Perhaps the novel should be read
       as a corollary to Plath's poetry because of the
       inescapable biographical material. The novel
       seems "a metaphor of an entire era suffocating
       under a bell jar."

28 LOCKE, RICHARD. "The Last Word: Beside The Bell
       Jar." New York Times (June 20, 1971), p.47
           Comments on the popularity of Sylvia Plath
       and The Bell Jar's rise to the bestseller list.

29 London Observer (November 21, 1971), p.10
           Editorial comment: A. Alvarez's memoir of
       Sylvia Plath excerpted from The Savage God will
       not be continued in the Observer "at the request
       of the Hughes family."

30 "Sylvia Plath Memoir Dropped." London Times (Novem-
       ber 19, 1971), p.14d
           Describes the conflict between A. Alvarez and
       the Hughes family over Alvarez's comments on
       Plath in The Savage God.

31 "Commentary." London Times Literary Supplement
       (November 19, 1971), p.1448
           Prints Ted Hughes' letter criticizing A. Al-
       varez's memoir of Sylvia Plath in The Savage
       God as distorted, misleading, spurious fantasiz-
       ing. "There is enough here to justify him and
       his publishers withdrawing the piece from wider
       circulation."

32 _____. London Times Literary Supplement (November
       26, 1971), p.1478
           Prints A. Alvarez's reply to Ted Hughes'
       letter claiming that Alvarez had distorted the
       facts of Plath's suicide. Alvarez defends him-
       self in terms of his right to say what he knew
       of the matter, the general publicity being given
       to Plath elsewhere, and that he was as delicate
       as possible in dealing with her suicide and
       other surrounding matters.

33 "At the End of the Line." <u>London Times Literary
    Supplement</u> (November 26, 1971), pp.1479-1480
        Comments on Alvarez's presentation of Plath.
    Alvarez's memoir "seems all the time to be leav-
    ing really important things unsaid."

34 "A World in Disintegration." <u>London Times Literary
    Supplement</u> (December 24, 1971), p.1602
        The poems in <u>Crossing the Water</u> and <u>Winter
    Trees</u> display Plath's movement away from the in-
    fluences of other poets into a new style and vo-
    cabulary. "One of the most noticeable aspects
    of that vocabulary is the way in which it en-
    ables discrete images to assume an internal
    relevance."

35 MADDOCKS, MELVIN. "A Vacuum Abhorred." <u>Christian
    Science Monitor</u> (April 15, 1971), p.11
        Biographical article on Plath, commenting on
    the autobiographical nature of <u>The Bell Jar</u> and
    some possible reasons for her great popularity.

36 MALOFF, SAUL. "Waiting for the Voice to Crack."
    <u>The New Republic</u>, CLIV (May 8, 1971), 33-35
        Reviews <u>The Bell Jar</u>. Sees the novel more
    as a journal and feels Plath's "Biographical
    Note" is "noteworthy." Comments particularly
    on the tone--influenced by Salinger. Summarizes
    some of the important incidents, often respond-
    ing negatively to Plath's manner of reporting
    them. Finally evaluates the novel as lacking in
    sufficient weight and complexity, placing <u>The
    Bell Jar</u> among Plath's juvenilia.

37 MEISSNER, WILLIAM. "The Rise of the Angel: Life
    Through Death in the Poetry of Sylvia Plath."
    <u>Massachusetts Studies in English</u>, III (1971),
    34-39
        Throughout Plath's work there is an "under-

MEISSNER, WILLIAM (cont.)
lying motif" of a recognition of chaos and a
searching for "spiritual purity." In her later
poems published in Ariel, Plath begins to sin-
cerely search for her "angel" through two primary methods: suffering and death. She is
capable of gaining both an objective and subjective view of herself and attempts to solve her
psychological trauma and desire for control by
the self-castigation presented in her work.

38 MELANDER, INGRID. "'The Disquieting Muses': A Note
on a Poem by Sylvia Plath." Research Studies
of Washington State University, XXXIX (March,
1971), 53-54
A discussion of the influence of Giorgio di
Chirico's painting "Le Muse Inquietanti" on
Plath's poem "The Disquieting Muses" (The Colossus). It is also noted that Plath's "On the
Decline of Oracles" uses as a motto a sentence
from a Chirico manuscript.

39 _____. "'Watercolor of Grantchester Meadows': An
Early Poem by Sylvia Plath." Moderna Språk,
LXV (1971), 1-5
A comment on Plath's "Watercolor of Grantchester Meadows," which is reprinted. The first
three stanzas of the poem present the landscape
features of the River Granta with very realistic
detail as a "quiet harmony." In the last
stanza, this harmony is reversed and nature becomes hostile and menacing.

40 MORSE, J. MITCHELL. "Fiction Chronicle." Hudson
Review, XXIV (Autumn, 1971), 537
The Bell Jar concerns Plath's shame at ac-
cepting and writing with false breathlessness
for a fashion magazine—something that "liter-

MORSE, J. MITCHELL (cont.)
ally made her sick." Plath "finally achieved a
more dignified feminine life. The Bell Jar is
the record of her struggle up from fashion, and
of her bad memories."

41 MOSS, HOWARD. "Dying: An Introduction." New
Yorker, XLVII (July 10, 1971), 73-75
The Bell Jar cannot be read as anything but
an autobiographical novel. Although "sickness
and disclosure" are the primary elements of the
book, they are not given to us as analyzed cri-
teria, but as "raw experience." Discusses vari-
ous details of Plath's life and a possible
connection between the novel and R. D. Laing's
clinical theories.

42 MURRAY, MICHELLE. "Prose and Cons." National Observer (May 31, 1971), p.18
The Bell Jar is an autobiographical novel
dealing with the subject of insanity in an
honest manner. Brief biographical details on
Plath are provided.

43 "The Bell Jar." Newsweek, LXXVII (April 19, 1971),
120
The Bell Jar "explains in the clearest possible way the inaccessibility of the psychotic."
Its force derives from the manner in which the
novel displays "the vulnerability of people of
hope and good will."

44 NYE, ROBERT. "A Bright Pane Broken." London Times
(September 30, 1971), p.12a
Sylvia Plath's work has produced a new freedom for contemporary poets. Briefly describes
the contents of Winter Trees.

45 O'HARA, JOHN. "An American Dream Girl." Washington
        Post (April 11, 1971), IX, p.8
            Brief discussion of The Bell Jar's history,
        Plath's life, and the peculiar qualities of The
        Bell Jar that allow it to escape easy delinea-
        tion.

46 PATERNO, DOMENICI. "Poetry." Library Journal, XCVI
        (October 1, 1971), 3141
            The Bell Jar displays Plath's ability and
        craft in portraying a character on the edge of
        psychological disintegration. Crossing the
        Water "deepens Plath's reputation for the talent
        to capture, and hold unflinchingly, death's apo-
        gean cold." "The Surgeon at 2 A.M." is re-
        printed from Crossing the Water.

47 The Poetry Book Society Bulletin, 70 (Autumn, 1971).
            Background detail for Winter Trees, The
        Poetry Book Society's selection for Autumn, 1971.
        Most of the remarks deal with "Three Women."

48 PORTER, PETER. "Collecting Her Strength." New
        Statesman, LXXXI (June 4, 1971), 774-775
            Crossing the Water is filled with "perfectly
        realized works." The poems represent Plath at a
        new, more complete realization of her talent.
        This volume is of equal stature and importance
        with The Colossus and Ariel.

49 "A Conversation With Robert Lowell." The Review, 26
        (Summer, 1971), 10-29
            Sylvia Plath is one of the four female poets
        in America that rank with the best male poets.
        "Years ago Sylvia and Anne Sexton audited my
        poetry class. Anne was more herself, and knew
        less. I thought they might rub off on each
        other. Sylvia learned from Anne."

50 RICHMOND, LEE J. "Books Covered and Uncovered."
        Erasmus Review, I (1971), 160-162
            The poems in Crossing the Water "move: both
        emotionally in the reader's response, and tech-
        nically in the buoyant, uninhibited cadence of
        her line as she attempts to speak her fever and
        chills with the truth of a dark vision."

51 ROSENTHAL, LUCY. "The Bell Jar." Saturday Review,
        LIV (April 24, 1971), 42
            Praises The Bell Jar as an "uncommonly fine
        piece of work," and despite the achievement of
        Ariel this work demands judgement in its own
        light. "With her classical restraint, Sylvia
        Plath is always refusing to break your heart,
        though in the end she breaks it anyway."

52 SARGEANT, HOWARD. "Poetry Review." English, XX
        (Autumn, 1971), 108
            Crossing the Water provides information on
        the transitional period in Plath's poetry be-
        tween the publications of The Colossus and
        Ariel. "In this volume it is possible to dis-
        cern how Sylvia Plath developed the command of
        language and the complicated metaphorical de-
        vices she was to use with such effect later; and
        at odd moments to catch her in the process of
        striving towards the emotional and psychological
        depths she had previously found in Lowell and
        Anne Sexton."

53 SCHOLES, ROBERT. "The Bell Jar." New York Times
        (April 11, 1971), VII, p.7
            The Bell Jar is a "fine novel" concerning
        life in the 1950's and what it is like to be in-
        sane. "Sylvia Plath has used superbly the most
        important technical device of realism"--defamil-
        iarization (making the world we know unfamiliar
        so it can be seen again).

54 SKELTON, ROBIN. "Poetry." Malahat Review, 20 (October, 1971), 137-138
The poems in Crossing the Water help to
justify Plath's reputation as a poet and also
display the same obsessive nature found in her
earlier published volumes. Her poetry is a
symptom of contemporary culture, where a dis-
trust of reason and order has produced a desire
for meaning to originate in mysticism and where
"the outcry is regarded as insight. . . . She
made her poetry a vision of the consequences of
that anti-intellectualism which surrounds us."
There are "dangerous distortions" in the philos-
ophy of Sylvia Plath.

55 STENGEL, E. "Poetry of Death." New Society,
XVIII (November 19, 1971), 997
In The Savage God, A. Alvarez's comments on
Sylvia Plath's suicide demonstrate that he
"shares a common misconception of what consti-
tutes a suicidal act." Most of those who com-
mit suicide "do not either want to die or to
live, but they want both at the same time,
usually one more, or much more, than the other."

56 STOIANOFF, ELLEN A. "Sylvia Plath." Mademoiselle,
LVIII (September, 1971), 160-161
Brief biographical summary of Plath's experi-
ence with Mademoiselle, recollections of those
who met her at that time, and three poems from
Crossing the Water: "The Surgeon at 2 A.M.,"
"Stillborn," and "Black Rook in Rainy Weather."

57 VENDLER, HELEN. "Crossing the Water." New York
Times (October 10, 1971), VII, pp.4, 48
Although Crossing the Water is not her best
work, it does show Plath in a transitional
period when she was maturing her own skill and
defining her point of view and freeing herself

VENDLER, HELEN (cont.)
from poetic influences. "In some way Sylvia
Plath sensed that her sensual or appetitive impulses were not the single-minded component she
would have liked them to be."

58 "Notes on Current Books." Virginia Quarterly Review, XLVII (Summer, 1971), xcvi
The Bell Jar is representative of the autobiographical nature of Plath's work. The novel
is of "superior quality."

59 WEINRARUR, BERNARD. "Literary Dispute Arises Over
Sylvia Plath's Death." New York Times (November 23, 1971), p.54
An account of the conflict between Ted Hughes
and A. Alvarez over the publication of Alvarez's chapter on Sylvia Plath in The Savage God.
Hughes says Alvarez's "'facts are material for
fiction, secondhand scraps, glimpses, half-ex-
periences, resurfacing after seven years, imaginatively reshaped.'"

A. Books--1972

1 MELANDER, INGRID. The Poetry of Sylvia Plath: A
Study of Themes. Stockholm: Almquist and Wik-
sell, 1972
A discussion of the major themes in Plath's
poetry. Her attitude toward nature, death, and
the image of her father are discussed in some
detail. There is also comment on Plath's pre-
occupation with the interrelated nature of
poetry and the graphic arts.

B. Articles--1972

1 AIRD, EILEEN M. "Variants in a Tape Recording of
     Fifteen Poems by Sylvia Plath." Notes and
     Queries, XIX (February, 1972), 59-61
       On October 30, 1962, Sylvia Plath made a re-
     cording of fifteen of her poems for the British
     Council series Contemporary Poets Reading Their
     Own Poems. Of these, two poems are still unpub-
     lished ("The Rabbit Catcher" and "A Secret") and
     only two are exactly the same as their pub-
     lished versions ("Daddy" and "A Birthday Pre-
     sent"). Variants in the other eleven poems are
     listed.

2 BAUMGAERTNER, JILL. "Four Poets: Blood Type New."
     Cresset, XXXVI (April, 1972), 16-17
       "Sylvia Plath's Winter Trees is a startling
     creation of richly violent images and uncanny
     insights peppered with black humor and bitter-
     ness and indented with soft bites of her special
     feminity."

3 "Best Books for Young Adults." Booklist, LXVIII
     (April 1, 1972), 664
       Brief plot synopsis of The Bell Jar.

4 CLUYSENAAR, ANNE. "Post-culture: Pre-culture?" in
     British Poetry Since 1960. Eds. Michael Schmidt
     and Grevel Lindop. Cheadle: Carcanet Press,
     1972, 213-232
       Sylvia Plath's poems show the psychological
     traits associated with "those who have, in some
     bodily or psychic sense, survived an experience
     of death," as described by Robert Jay Lifton in
     Death in Life: The Survivors of Hiroshima. With

CLUYSENAAR, ANNE (cont.)
Ted Hughes, Plath is one of the two "extreme re-
presentatives" of British poetry in the 1960's
demonstrating a dual crisis (emotional and intellectual) in contemporary culture.

5 DAVIS, WILLIAM V. "Sylvia Plath's 'Ariel.'" Modern
Poetry Studies, III (1972), 176-184
The title of Sylvia Plath's poem "Ariel" has
a threefold meaning. First, on a biographical
level, Ariel is the name of a horse which she
rode weekly. Second, Ariel refers to Shake-
speare's The Tempest. Third, it is the symbolic
name for Jerusalem. Of these, the biographical
and biblical are the most important.

6 DAVISON, PETER. "Three Visionary Poets." Atlantic,
CCXXIX (February, 1972), 104-106
In the poems in Crossing the Water, Plath
sets "her eye and her heart at loggerheads."
In Ariel, this conflict is resolved and Plath's
vision becomes unified. Her dedication "as an
artist was as total as her humanity was defec-
tive."

7 DUNN, DOUGLAS. "King Offa Alive and Dead." Encounter, XXXVIII (January, 1972), 67
In Winter Trees, "it is the mood—collective-
ly, of all the poems—that is so impressive.
. . . Life is absorbed into art, yet remains
active in the poems, raw and enigmatical."

8 GORDON, JAN B. "Saint Sylvia." Modern Poetry
Studies, III (1972), 282-286
Winter Trees demonstrates Plath's withdrawal
from life, the desolation in the landscape of
her vision, and her tendency to see herself as
a mystic and a martyr. "We are now in the midst

GORDON, JAN B. (cont.)
of a Sylvia Plath myth, a veritable saint's life
whose relics Ted Hughes brings out every year or
so for our communal worship in the role of edi-
tor-historian-biographer who has the keys to the
kingdom."

9 GRANT, DAMIAN. "Reviews and Comment." Critical
   Quarterly, XIV (Spring, 1972), 92-94
   Although Winter Trees is the smallest of
   Plath's posthumous collections, "there is ample
   further evidence of her endless imaginative re-
   sources in the restatement of her familiar
   themes." "Three Women" is clearly the most important piece in the volume.

10 HOBSBAUM, PHILIP. "The Temptations of Giant De-
    spair." Hudson Review, XXV (Winter, 1972-1973),
    597-612
    Deals with the distortion of Sylvia Plath's
    life and work by A. Alvarez (The Savage God),
    John Berryman, and Anne Sexton. When Plath's
    poetry is compared to Lowell, her narrow range
    is made clear, although she is better than Sex-
    ton or Berryman. "The Savage God is a personal
    exploration of a painful terrain in which Sylvia
    Plath figures as heroine and Mr. Alvarez himself
    as a spectator on the sidelines."

11 HOLBROOK, DAVID. Dylan Thomas: The Code of the
    Night. London: The Athlone Press University of
    London, 1972
    Throughout Holbrook's study, Plath is men-
    tioned as "learning" from Thomas' experiences
    and comparable to him in poetic content.

12 HOWE, IRVING. "Sylvia Plath: A Partial Disagree-
       ment." Harper's, CCXLIV (January, 1972), 88-91
          Refers to The Colossus, Crossing the Water,
       Ariel. Comments on the biographical limitations
       of Plath's confessional poetry, tracing the in-
       fluence of Robert Lowell's Life Studies on her
       lyrics, and indicating his generally successful
       objectification of experience in his poetry in
       contradistinction to Plath's usual inability to
       achieve more than personal revelation. Howe
       believes her "notable gift" is to draw the
       "single, isolated image," but her weakness occurs
       through excess. He believes her to be fragment-
       ed and lacking "controlled maturity of con-
       sciousness." He relegates her to the position
       of a future anthologized minor poet, devaluing
       her for lack of vision. Mentions his response
       is basically to The Art of Sylvia Plath, ed.
       Charles Newman (Indiana University Press).

13 HOWES, VICTOR. "Sometimes a Walker of Air." Chris-
       tian Science Monitor (October 4, 1972), 11
          Plath speaks in the poems in Winter Trees as
       the personal voice of a mother addressing her
       husband and children. Her poems deserve to be
       read as if they are anonymous; it would then be
       possible to see more in her poetry, "as drama-
       tizations, not autobiographical fragments."

14 JENNINGS, CAROL. "The Woman Poet." New York Quar-
       terly, 12 (Autumn, 1972), 123-126
          Briefly mentions Plath's popular appeal and
       quotes from "Lesbos" and "Three Women." With
       Sexton, Plath did the most to "'legitimatize'
       the female experience."

15 KRAMER, VICTOR. "Life-and-Death Dialectics."
      Modern Poetry Studies, III (1972), 40-42
          The poems in Crossing the Water allow the
      reader to perceive the transition in Plath's
      work in the time between the publications of
      The Colossus and Ariel. "These poems demon-
      strate that she became stronger as poet, while
      her awareness became more intense." Mentions
      Stevens and Roethke as possible influences.

16 Kirkus Reviews, XL (July 15, 1972), 846
          The conflict between the Heraclitean and
      Freudian strains is resolved in a "fusion"
      which gives "real 'meaning'" to the poems in
      Winter Trees.

17 _____, XL (August 15, 1972), 956
          Reprint of the review in Kirkus Reviews of
      July 15, 1972

18 LASK, THOMAS. "Autumn Yields Rich Harvest of Verse."
      New York Times (September 7, 1972), p.52
          Mentions the publication of Winter Trees.

19 MEGNA, JEROME. "Plath's 'Manor Garden.'" The Ex-
      plicator, XXX (March, 1972), No. 58
          In Plath's "Manor Garden" many of the themes
      of The Colossus are presented. "The movement of
      the poem is from aridity to fertility, from
      death to life, from complete lack of motion to
      a great convergence."

20 MURRAY, MICHELLE. "Okay, Sylvia Plath Was Good, but
      Not That Good." National Observer (September
      30, 1972), p.27
          Discusses the general course of Plath's
      career, her suicide, her subsequent fame, and

MURRAY, MICHELLE (cont.)
    her major themes. Most of the poems in Winter
    Trees do not possess the quality of her later
    work in Ariel, except possibly "Mystic" and
    "Winter Trees."

21 NEWLIN, MARGARET. "The Suicide Bandwagon." Criti-
    cal Quarterly, XIV (Winter, 1972), 367-378
        Sylvia Plath has become the center of what
    A. Alvarez terms the "extremists," those who
    take ultimate risks moving at the edge of life
    and death. But her followers—notably Anne Sex-
    ton and Alvarez—have diminished in their own
    work the intensity that is felt in Plath's.
    Plath's contribution was in not freeing the poet
    to write more and more explanations of the tor-
    tured "extremist" psyche, but "a kind of libera-
    tion from having to express those self-destruc-
    tive tendencies she articulated so definitively,
    and a freeing, perhaps, into a new poetry of
    survival."

22 "Reference Books." New York Quarterly, 12 (Autumn,
    1972), 110-111
        Plath's Ariel is recommended as "indispens-
    able reading for the practicing poet."

23 OATES, JOYCE CAROL. "Poetry." Library Journal, XCV
    (November 1, 1972), 3595
        The poems in Winter Trees are not as striking
    as those in Ariel, but a number, especially
    "Three Women," are "unforgettable for their
    eerie fusion of power and helplessness." These
    poems "reveal the dissolving of the ego," a lack
    of sexual identity. In their concerns with the
    dissolution of the poet's personality, these
    poems are outstanding.

24 OBERG, ARTHUR. "The Modern British and American
       Lyric: What Will Suffice?" Language and Litera-
       ture, VII (Winter, 1972), 70-88
         "Things proliferate in Sylvia Plath's poems
       in the way they do in an Ionesco play or Antoni-
       oni movie. The Ariel poems, by being essential-
       ly about love and language, indicate how far
       image and object have polarized and how great
       an effort the poet must bring with him in coming
       to his world." Plath's reliance on the image
       brings disintegration.

25 PERLOFF, MARJORIE. "'A Ritual for Being Born Twice':
       Sylvia Plath's The Bell Jar." Contemporary
       Literature, XII (Autumn, 1972), 507-522
         Psychological discussion of The Bell Jar in
       terms of R. D. Laing's The Divided Self. The
       novel is a portrayal of Esther Summerson's
       gradual evolvement toward a new approach for
       coping with existence. The progress is com-
       pounded by disease, which is symbolically used
       to provide "an index to the human inability to
       cope with an unlivable situation." Brief com-
       parison to McCullers' The Member of the Wedding
       and Ibsen's A Doll's House.

26 PHILLIPS, ROBERT. "The Dark Funnel: A Reading of
       Sylvia Plath." Modern Poetry Studies, III
       (1972), 49-74
         Throughout Plath's work there is a pervasive
       theme dealing with the death and rejection of
       the father figure. The father becomes the chief
       archetypal configuration (Jungian sense) with
       which Plath identifies, making her into a
       "modern Electra."

27 PRITCHARD, WILLIAM H. "Youngsters, Middlesters, and
       Some Old Boys." Hudson Review, XXV (Spring,
       1972), 124
          The best of the poems in Crossing the Water
       "put the reader at a great and artful distance"
       from the poet. "At their best they move beyond
       society, irony and tone of voice to the realm
       of something else."

28 Publishers' Weekly, CCI (February 28, 1972), 74
          The Bell Jar is an autobiographical novel.

29 "The State of Poetry--A Symposium." The Review, 29-
       30 (Spring-Summer, 1972), 3-73
          A series of comments by contemporary poets
       on the present situation of poetry. Plath is
       mentioned throughout.

30 ROSENSTEIN, HARRIET. "Reconsidering Sylvia Plath."
       Ms., I (September, 1972), 44-57, 96-98
          General appraisal of Plath's work, especially
       The Bell Jar and Ariel. Heavy reliance on these
       works' autobiographical elements.

31 "Books: Shorter Reviews." Saturday Review, LXXXIII
       (October 28, 1972), 83
          The poems in Winter Trees are extraordinary,
       displaying Plath's original talent.

32 SCHMIDT, MICHAEL AND GREVEL LINDOP, EDS. British
       Poetry Since 1960. Cheadle: Carcanet Press,
       1972, 74, 143, 207, 216, 219, 226, 241, 243
          Plath is mentioned in several of the essays
       in this survey. At times, she is an influence
       and, at other times, an extreme example of the
       currents seen in contemporary British poetry.
       See Anne Cluysenaar's "Post-culture: Pre-cul-
       ture?" for the most extended discussion of Plath.

33 SMITH, PAMELA. "The Unitive Urge in the Poetry of
      Sylvia Plath." New England Quarterly, XLV
      (September, 1972), 323-339
        Throughout Plath's work there is a constant
      drive for total unity, a resolution of con-
      flicting opposites experienced as a battle be-
      tween the self and that which is outside the
      self. In her poetry, she gradually begins to
      take a more overt and intimate notice of the
      contradictory elements in her life. Her meta-
      phors become more intense and her subject mat-
      ter more extreme. The influences of Roethke,
      Hughes, Sexton, Lowell and the popular accep-
      tance of the confessional style are discussed.

34 SMITH, RAYMOND. "Late Harvest." Modern Poetry
      Studies, III (1972), 91-93
        The poems in Winter Trees are not completely
      finished. No doubt some of these poems would
      have been discarded, transformed or revised had
      Plath lived to collect them into a book herself.
      They do present Plath at her best and, with
      "Three Women," are especially concerned with re-
      lations between the sexes.

35 SPACKS, PATRICIA MEYER. "A Chronicle of Women."
      Hudson Review, XXV (Spring, 1972), 163-166
        In The Bell Jar, "Plath's writing is often
      school-girlish," but its effect on the reader is
      like an "electrocution." Plath's novel is com-
      pared to Sandra Hochman's Walking Papers, Joan
      Haggerty's Daughters of the Moon, and Julia
      O'Faolain's Three Lovers.

36 STOREY, ELIZABETH. "Non-Fiction." Library Journal,
      XCVII (January 15, 1973), 276
        The poems in Winter Trees are primarily con-

STOREY, ELIZABETH (cont.)
cerned with death and "project a depressing
morbidity." The subject matter is common, but
the method is unique.

37 "Notes on Current Books." Virginia Quarterly Review, XLVIII (Winter, 1972), xxii
The poems in Crossing the Water speak to all
mankind.

A. Books--1973

1 AIRD, EILEEN. Sylvia Plath. New York: Barnes and
Noble, 1973
After a biographical and critical introduction which outlines Plath's career, Aird pro-
vides chapter-length discussions of The Colossus,
Crossing the Water, Winter Trees, Ariel, The
Bell Jar, and Plath's use of imagery. She also
comments on the influences of Robert Lowell,
Anne Sexton, and Theodore Roethke on her work
and the relationship between Plath's poetry and
that of Ted Hughes.

2 STEINER, NANCY HUNTER. A Closer Look at Ariel: A
Memory of Sylvia Plath. New York: Harper's
Magazine Press, 1973
A memoir of the author's friendship with Sylvia Plath at Smith College and during one summer
at Harvard. The closing pages deal with her reaction to Plath's death.

B. Articles--1973

1 "Literature." <u>Booklist</u>, LXIX (January 1, 1973), 424
      Most of the poems in <u>Winter Trees</u> reflect
      Plath's maturing style during the time between
      the publication of <u>The Colossus</u> and <u>Ariel</u>.

2 "Books for Young Adults." <u>Booklist</u>, LXIX (January
      15, 1973), 490
      <u>Winter Trees</u> demonstrates Plath's preoccupa-
      tion with death.

3 <u>Choice</u>, IX (February, 1973), 1592
      "In <u>Winter Trees</u>, Plath has reached the apex
      of her art."

4 COOLEY, PETER. "Autism, Autoeroticism, Auto-da-fe:
      The Tragic Poetry of Sylvia Plath." <u>Hollins
      Critic</u>, X (February, 1973), 1-15
      The poems in <u>The Colossus</u> display Plath's
      early willingness to commit herself to the ex-
      tremes demonstrated in her later work, and they
      show her to be "among the first of her genera-
      tion to admit her fear of the existential pro-
      cess itself." In <u>Crossing the Water</u>, the reader
      can see Plath beginning to take a more forth-
      right stance and her attempt to move away from
      former influences (Lowell, Wilbur, and Roethke).
      In <u>Ariel</u>, Plath's achievement is found. "Her
      world is cut on a fundamental life-death dichot-
      omy which severely restricts and intensifies it."

5 COTTER, JAMES FINN. "Women Poets: Malign Neglect?"
      <u>America</u>, CXXVIII (February 17, 1973), 140
      Comments on Plath's overnight popularity aft-
      er the publication of <u>Ariel</u> and her image as
      "the embattled heroine of the Women's Liberation
      Movement." <u>Winter Trees</u> will enhance her repu-
      tation and increase "a new self-awareness for
      women."

6 DUNN, DOUGLAS. "Mechanics of Misery." Encounter,
     XLI (August, 1973), 84–85
        Notes the influence of Plath's poetry on
     Erica Jong's Fruits and Vegetables.

7 HASSAN, IHAB. Contemporary American Literature:
     1945–1972. New York: Frederick Ungar, 1973,
     103, 132–133
        Plath "writes verse of grotesque power and
     originality, macabre in its badinage, bloody in
     laying the soul bare." Her work attempts to
     manipulate the external world in search for re-
     newal. Compared to Allen Ginsberg in the manner
     that both he and Plath tend to assume the diffi-
     culties of the world onto the self.

8 HOWARD, RICHARD. "Five Poets." Poetry, CCXXI
     (October, 1973), 54–55
        Reprinted from Poetry, March, 1973

9 KAMEEN, PAUL. Best Sellers, XXXII (January 15,
     1973), 474–475
        Review of Winter Trees. Plath's poetry re-
     lies on the manipulation of reality by the
     poet's subjective response. "It was precisely
     her omnipresent, inescapable ego that was the
     essence of her poetic gift."

10 MARVEL, BILL. "Unsung in Life, Lionized in Death."
     National Observer, XII (February 10, 1973), 1,
     18
        Discussion of the cult of adulation surround-
     ing Plath, Eva Hesse, and Diane Arbus. These
     three contemporaries are seen as "manufactured"
     martyrs reflecting the spirit of alienation and
     frustration in American society during the
     1960's and early 1970's.

11 OATES, JOYCE CAROL. "The Death Throes of Romanti-
      cism: The Poems of Sylvia Plath." Southern Re-
      view, IX (July, 1973), 501-522
          "This essay is an attempt to analyze Miss
      Plath in terms of her cultural significance, to
      diagnose through her poetry the pathological
      aspects of our era which makes a death of the
      spirit inevitable--for that era and for all who
      believe in its assumptions." As the title
      states, the era is Romanticism, and Sylvia
      Plath's poetry is indicative of its last stage.
      The problem of the Romantic is the irresolvable
      tension between subject and object, which
      causes, for those who accept its "assumptions,"
      a circular self-defeating preoccupation with the
      self and its inferiority when faced with the
      enemy of the Other, the not-self. Oates feels
      that the circular arguments of the Romantic and
      the ultimate destructiveness that is displayed
      in Plath's work will be replaced by a new sense
      of the unity and totality of man with the world
      outside of the self.

12 PERLOFF, MARJORIE. "On the Road to Ariel: The
      'Transitional' Poetry of Sylvia Plath." Iowa
      Review, IV (Spring, 1973), 94-110
          In the context of Crossing the Water and Win-
      ter Trees, Ariel loses some of the impact it
      originally possessed: "one begins to speculate
      that perhaps, in the case of Sylvia Plath's
      poetry, less is more. The lyric intensity of
      her vision somehow seems more impressive when
      one first meets it in the slim rigorously selec-
      tive Ariel than when it is placed in the per-
      spective afforded by the publication of her un-
      collected poems." Her poetic concerns are too
      narrow, but her effect, through a rather small
      number of poems that show new ways beyond the

85

PERLOFF, MARJORIE (cont.)
work of Lowell, Roethke, and Lawrence, on young-
er poets is still great. Perloff is quick to
show that the poems in Crossing the Water are
inaccurately described as "transitional" (many
being published in The Colossus period) and that
in this volume and Winter Trees the editorial
process is ambiguously motivated and quite mis-
leading.

13 PEVEAR, RICHARD. "Poetry Chronicle." Hudson Review, XXVI (Spring, 1973), 208-209
The poems in Winter Trees portray Plath's
view of nothingness everywhere. "Mallarme and
Reverdy both undertook their combat-in-secret in
order to defest the demonic monsters and de-
liver the world's reality. Sylvia Plath's
images are set off against nothing, they are
images of the nullity in things, and that is
what makes them uncanny."

14 PHILLIPS, ROBERT. The Confessional Poets. Carbon-
dale: Southern Illinois University Press, 1973,
6-14, 128-152
Reprints Phillips' "The Dark Funnel: A Reading of Sylvia Plath" from Modern Poetry Studies.
In the first chapter of the book, "The Confessional Mode in Modern American Poetry," Phillips
traces some of the themes and characteristics
common among confessional poets.

15 PRATT, LINDA RAY. "'The spirit of blackness is in
us . . .'" Prairie Schooner, XLVII (Spring,
1973), 87-90
The Bell Jar is Plath's early and unsatisfac-
tory novel which never goes below the surface of
its materials. In Winter Trees and Crossing the

PRATT, LINDA RAY (cont.)
Water, the writing is more satisfactory. The
first volume shows "the stunning intensity and
originality of her best poems." The second
helps the reader to understand Plath in the
period preceding Ariel.

16 SMITH, PAMELA. "Architectonics: Sylvia Plath's
Colossus." Ariel, IV (January, 1973), 4-21
The division in Plath's work between The
Colossus and Ariel has become widely accepted,
but this division is superficial and fails to
recognize the unity of her work. In The Colossus, Plath was very much concerned with method
and technique and in exploring what she knew
about poetic tradition. In Ariel, Plath's poems
build upon her earlier explorations. Extensive
comments are made in regard to Plath's poetics
and the critical response—especially Frederick
Nims' article "The Poetry of Sylvia Plath: A
Technical Analysis"—to her first book.

17 STADE, GEORGE. "Introduction" in A Closer Look at
Ariel: A Memory of Sylvia Plath. New York:
Harper's Magazine Press, 1973, 3-30
Attempts to relate Plath's biography with her
poetry and The Bell Jar. The importance of
Steiner's A Closer Look At Ariel is that it pro-
vides details that are not found in other sources
on Plath and, therefore, helps in understanding
Plath's work more fully. Extensive reference to
Plath's works.

18 STEINER, NANCY HUNTER. "Sylvia Plath: A Roommate's
Memoir." Mademoiselle (January, 1973), 96-100
A remembrance of Plath during one summer in
college. Originally published in Steiner's A
Closer Look at Ariel.

Writings by Anne Sexton

Poetry--1958

1 "Just Once." Audience, V (August, 1958), 35-40

2 "The Exorcists." Audience, V (August, 1958), 35-40

3 "Hutch." Audience, V (August, 1958), 35-40

4 "The Bells." Audience, V (August, 1958), 35-40

5 "And That's the Way It Was." Audience, V (August, 1958), 35-40

6 "Didn't Know." Beloit Poetry Journal, VII (Summer, 1958), 17

Poetry--1959

1 "The Farmer's Wife." Harper's, CCXVIII (May, 1959), 60

2 "Double Image." Hudson Review, XII (Spring, 1959), 73-81

3 "You, Doctor Martin." Hudson Review, XII (Spring, 1959), 73-81

4 "Elizabeth Gone." Hudson Review, XII (Spring, 1959), 73-81

BY ANNE SEXTON (1959)

5   "The Lost Ingredient." <u>Yale Review</u>, XLVIII (June, 1959), 559

6   "Sunbathers." <u>New Yorker</u>, XXXV (June 13, 1959), 93

7   "Noon Walk on the Asylum Lawn." <u>Voices</u>, 169 (May-August, 1959), 34

8   "Obsessive Combination of Ontological Inscape, Trickery, and Love." <u>Voices</u>, 169 (May-August, 1959), 34

9   "Lullaby." <u>Audience</u>, VI (August, 1959), 28-32

10 "The Moss of His Skin." <u>Audience</u>, VI (August, 1959), 28-32

11 "What's That." <u>Audience</u>, VI (August, 1959), 28-32

12 "Elegy in the Classroom." <u>Audience</u>, VI (August, 1959), 28-32

13 "Her Kind." <u>Audience</u>, VI (August, 1959), 28-32

14 "The Road Back." <u>New Yorker</u>, XXXV (August 29, 1959), 30

15 "For Johnny Pole on the Forgotten Beach." <u>Antioch Review</u>, XIX (Fall, 1959), 360-361

16 "My Friend, My Friend." <u>Antioch Review</u>, XIX (Fall, 1959), 360-361

17 "Kind Sir: These Woods." <u>Harper's</u>, CCXIX (November, 1959), 40

BY ANNE SEXTON (1959)

18   "Where I Live in This Honorable House of the Laurel Tree." Epoch, IX (Winter, 1959), 171-172

19   "The Waiting Head." Epoch, IX (Winter, 1959), 171-172

20   "Torn Down From Glory Daily." Accent, XIX (Winter, 1959), 19-21

21   "Portrait of an Old Woman on the College Tavern Wall." Accent, XIX (Winter, 1959), 19-21

22   "Division of Parts." Hudson Review, XII (Winter, 1959), 537-544

23   "Music Swims Back to Me." Hudson Review, XII (Winter, 1959), 537-544

24   "Expatriates." Hudson Review, XII (Winter, 1959), 537-544

25   "A Story for Rose on the Midnight Flight to Boston." Hudson Review, XII (Winter, 1959), 537-544

Book--1960

1   To Bedlam and Part Way Back. Boston: Houghton Mifflin, 1960

Prose--1960

1   "Dancing the Jig" in New World Writing, Number 16. New York: New American Library, 1960, 146-153

BY ANNE SEXTON (1960)

Poetry—1960

1 "Ringing the Bells." Nation, CXC (March 12, 1960), 231

2 "Some Foreign Letters." Partisan Review, XXVII (Spring, 1960), 272-275

3 "Said the Poet to the Analyst." Saturday Review, XLIII (September 3, 1960), 18

4 "Dear Alumna: So That We May Complete Our Records." Poetry Northwest, I (Winter, 1960), 23-26

5 "Funnel." Poetry Northwest, I (Winter, 1960), 23-26

6 "The Kite." Poetry Northwest, I (Winter, 1960), 23-26

Poetry—1961

1 "All My Pretty Ones." Hudson Review, XIV (Spring, 1961), 20-27

2 "I Remember." Hudson Review, XIV (Spring, 1961), 20-27

3 "Old Dwarf Heart." Hudson Review, XIV (Spring, 1961), 20-27

4 "The Truth the Dead Know." Hudson Review, XIV (Spring, 1961), 20-27

5 "Young." Hudson Review, XIV (Spring, 1961), 20-27

6 "Letter Written on a Ferry While Crossing Long Island Sound." New Yorker, XXXVII (June 10, 1961), 34

BY ANNE SEXTON (1961)

7 "Starry Night." Nation, CXCIII (September 2, 1961),
     126

8 "A Curse Against Elegies." Partisan Review, XXVIII
     (September-November, 1961), 605-611

9 "For God While Sleeping." Partisan Review, XXVIII
     (September-November, 1961), 605-611

10 "In the Deep Museum." Partisan Review, XXVIII (Sep-
     tember-November, 1961), 605-611

11 "Ghosts." Partisan Review, XXVIII (September-Novem-
     ber, 1961), 605-611

12 "The Abortion." Partisan Review, XXVIII (September-
     November, 1961), 605-611

13 "With Mercy for the Greedy." Partisan Review,
     XXVIII (September-November, 1961), 605-611

14 "To a Friend Whose Work Has Come to Triumph."
     Harper's, CCXXIII (November, 1961), 93

15 "The House." Poetry, XCIX (December, 1961), 160-163

Book--1962

1 All My Pretty Ones. Boston: Houghton Mifflin, 1962

Prose--1962

1 "Some Foreign Letters" in Poet's Choice. Eds. Paul
     Engle and Joseph Langland. New York: Dial Press
     1962, 274-277. (Reprints "Some Foreign Letters,"
     which is followed by Sexton's comments on the
     poem.)

BY ANNE SEXTON (1962)

Poetry--1962

1 "The Sun." New Yorker, XXXVIII (May, 1962), 44

2 "From the Garden." Poetry, C (August, 1962), 271-277

3 "Wallflower." Poetry, C (August, 1962), 271-277

4 "Woman With Girdle." Poetry, C (August, 1962), 271-277

5 "For Eleanor Boylan Talking With God." Poetry, C (August, 1962), 271-277

6 "The Black Art." Poetry, C (August, 1962), 271-277

7 "Old." Poetry, C (August, 1962), 271-277

8 "Water." Poetry, C (August, 1962), 271-277

9 "Lament." Literary Review, V (Summer, 1962), 560

10 "Letter Written During a January Northeaster." Hudson Review, XV (Summer, 1962), 228-235

11 "Doors, Doors, Doors." Hudson Review, XV (Summer, 1962), 228-235

12 "Hangman." Hudson Review, XV (Summer, 1962), 228-235

13 "Love Song for K. Owyne." Hudson Review, XV (Summer, 1962), 228-235

14 "Starry Night." Nation, CXCIII (September 2, 1962), 126

BY ANNE SEXTON (1962)

15 "Fortress." New Yorker, XXXVIII (September 22, 1962), 44

16 "Mother and Jack and the Rain." Harper's, CCV (October, 1962), 153

17 "Somewhere in Africa." Poetry, CI (October, 1962), 113

18 "Flight" in Poetry Supplement. Ed. W. S. Merwin. London: The Poetry Book Society, 1962

Book--1963

1 Eggs of Things. New York: G. P. Putnam, 1963. (With Maxine Kumin.)

Prose--1963

1 "The Last Believer." Vogue, CXLII (November 15, 1963), 76

Poetry--1963

1 "And One For My Dame." Carleton Miscellany, IV (Spring, 1963), 41-44

2 "Consorting With Angels." Carleton Miscellany, IV (Spring, 1963), 41-44

3 "Love Song." Harper's, CCXXVII (October, 1963), 83

BY ANNE SEXTON (1964)

Book—1964

1 Selected Poems. London: Oxford University Press, 1964

Poetry—1964

1 "Sylvia's Death." Poetry, CIII (June, 1964), 224-226

2 "Three Green Windows." New Yorker, XL (June 6, 1964), 44

3 "Christmas Eve." Critical Quarterly, VI (Summer, 1964), 103-106

4 "Those Times. . . ." Critical Quarterly, VI (Summer, 1964), 103-106

5 "The Legend of the One-Eyed Man." Sewanee Review, LXXII (Summer, 1964), 449-451

Poetry—1965

1 "KE 6-8018." Poetry, CVI (April, 1965), 116-119

2 "The Wedding Night." Poetry, CVI (April, 1965), 116-119

3 "Two Sons." Hudson Review, XVIII (Spring, 1965), 45-53

4 "To Lose the Earth." Hudson Review, XVIII (Spring, 1965), 45-53

5 "Menstruation." Hudson Review, XVIII (Spring, (1965), 45-53

BY ANNE SEXTON (1965)

6 "Imitations of Drowning." Hudson Review, XVIII
      (Spring, 1965), 45-53

7 "Crossing the Atlantic." Hudson Review, XVIII
      (Spring 1965), 45-53

8 "For the Year of the Insane: A Prayer." Harper's,
      CCXXX (June, 1965), 68

9 "Little Girl, My Stringbean, My Lovely Woman." New
      Yorker, XLI (August 7, 1965), 30

10 "You, Doctor Martin." Critical Quarterly Poetry
      Supplement Number Six (1965), 8-10

11 "Sylvia's Death." Critical Quarterly Poetry Supple-
      ment Number Six (1965), 8-10

Book--1966

1 Live Or Die. Boston: Houghton Mifflin, 1966

Prose--1966

1 "The Barfly Ought to Sing." Tri-Quarterly, 7 (Fall,
      1966), 89-94

Poetry--1966

1 "Pain for a Daughter." New Yorker, XLII (March 26,
      1966), 50

2 "Flee on Your Donkey." New Yorker, XLII (May 7,
      1966), 44-45

3   "Two Suns." Agenda, IV (Summer, 1966), 24-26

4   "To Lose the Earth." Agenda, IV (Summer, 1966), 24-
    26

5   "Protestant Easter." Tri-Quarterly, 6 (Summer,
    1966), 79-90

6   "Man and Wife." Tri-Quarterly, 6 (Summer, 1966),
    79-90

7   "Cripples and Other Stories." Tri-Quarterly, 6
    (Fall, 1966), 79-90

8   "The Addict." Tri-Quarterly, 6 (Summer, 1966), 79-
    90

9   "Suicide Note." Tri-Quarterly, 6 (Summer, 1966),
    79-90

10 "Your Face on the Dog's Neck." New Yorker, XLII
    (September 3, 1966), 40

Poetry--1967

1   "The Nude Swim." Harper's, CCXXXV (December, 1967),
    107

2   "The Touch." New American Review. New York: New
    American Library, 1967, 49-50

Poetry--1968

1   "For My Lover, Returning to His Wife." New Yorker,
    XLIV (February 3, 1968), 91

Sylvia Plath and Anne Sexton: A Reference Guide

BY ANNE SEXTON (1968)

2 "It Is a Spring Afternoon." New Yorker, XLIV
       (April 27, 1968), 48

3 "Interrogation of the Man of Many Hearts." Hudson
       Review, XXI (Spring, 1968), 99–106

4 "Ballad of the Lonely Masturbator." Hudson Review,
       XXI (Spring, 1968), 99–106

5 "The Break." Hudson Review, XXI (Spring, 1968), 99–
       106

6 "The Breast." Critical Quarterly, X (Spring–Summer,
       1968), 111–112

7 "Days Without You." New Yorker, XLIV (June 29,
       1968), 34–35

8 "Moon Song." New Yorker, XLIV (September 7, 1968),
       32

9 "Us." New Yorker, XLIV (November 23, 1968), 58

10 "You All Know the Story About the Other Woman." At-
       lantic, CCXXII (November, 1968), 81

11 "With You Gone." Critical Quarterly, X (Winter,
       1968), 385–392

12 "In Celebration of My Uterus." Quarterly Review of
       Literature, XVI (1968), 216–219

13 "Kiss." Quarterly Review of Literature, XVI (1968),
       216–219

14 "Song for a Red Nightgown." Quarterly Review of
       Literature, XVI (1968), 216–219

Sylvia Plath and Anne Sexton: A Reference Guide

BY ANNE SEXTON (1968)

Worksheets--1968

1 "Anne Sexton: Worksheets." <u>Malahat Review</u>, VI
     (1968), 105-114

Book--1969

1 <u>Love Poems</u>. Boston: Houghton Mifflin, 1969

Poetry--1969

1 "Moon Song, Woman Song." <u>New York Times</u> (July 21,
     1969, p.17

Drama--1969

1 "Mercy Street."
       Performed at the American Place Theater in
  New York; opening night on October 27, 1969; unpublished.

Books--1971

1 <u>Joey and the Birthday Present</u>. New York: McGraw-
     Hill, 1971. (With Maxine Kumin.)

2 <u>Transformations</u>. Boston: Houghton Mifflin, 1971

Poetry--1971

1 "The Little Peasant." <u>Playboy</u>, XVIII (January,
     1971), 197

BY ANNE SEXTON (1971)

2 "The Maiden Without Hands." Audience, I (January-
  February, 1971), 25-26

3 "Iron Hans." Audience, I (January-February, 1971),
  25-26

4 "Snow White and the Seven Dwarfs." Cosmopolitan,
  CLXXVI (April, 1971), 86, 90

5 "Hansel and Gretel." Cosmopolitan, CLXXVII (April,
  1971), 84

6 "Ambition Bird." Saturday Review, LIV (August 14,
  1971), 54-55

7 "For Mr. Death Who Stands With His Door Open."
  Saturday Review, LIV (August 14, 1971), 54-55

8 "Doctor of the Heart." Saturday Review, LIV
  (August 14, 1971), 18-19

9 "The Boat." New Yorker, XLVII (August, 1971), 30

10 "The Wedlock." New Republic, CLXV (December 11,
   1971), 23

Writings about Anne Sexton

A. Books—1960

None

B. Articles—1960

1 BAGG, ROBERT. "A Regime of Revelation." <u>Audience</u>,
      VII (Summer, 1960), 121-125
          Sexton's poetry makes more demands upon the
      reader than is usual, as well as demanding more
      from the poet. Her poems in <u>To Bedlam and Part
      Way Back</u> "are suggestive without being sym-
      bolic," and thereby avoid certain dangers.
      Lowell and Snodgrass created the climate from
      which Sexton's works result.

2 HARTMANN, GEOFFREY. "Les Belles Dames Sans Merci."
      <u>Kenyon Review</u>, XXII (Autumn, 1960), 697-699
          <u>To Bedlam and Part Way Back</u> is not Sexton's
      search for self-knowledge, but a summoning of
      courage prior to the search itself. The experi-
      ence described is universalized and concerns
      facing "a Mode of Being fatally estranged from
      her."

3 HOWES, BARBARA. "Voice of a New Poet." <u>New York
      Herald-Tribune</u> (December 11, 1960), p.37
          <u>To Bedlam and Part Way Back</u> conveys a "real
      sense of personality" to the reader. Although

HOWES, BARBARA (cont.)
some of the poems are unsuccessful and the title
ill-chosen, Sexton has made an "honest and impressive achievement."

4 MEYERS, NEIL. "The Hungry Sheep Look Up." Minne-
sota Review, I (October, 1960), 99-104
The poems in To Bedlam and Part Way Back rely
on accurate observation, a specified location,
and a story. Sexton's poems are about experience, rather than attempting to be experience.
Contrasts her poetry to Robert Lowell's.

5 SMITH, HAL. "Notes, Reviews and Speculations."
Epoch, X (Fall, 1960), 253-255
To Bedlam and Part Way Back contains poems
that "are naked of fiction." "Perhaps this
plainess is the hope for poetry; perhaps we
need a poet who is willing to look at her dis-
asters" in an honest manner.

A. Books--1961

None

B. Articles--1961

1 DICKEY, JAMES. "Five First Books." Poetry, XCVII
(February, 1961), 318-319. Reprinted in Babel
to Byzantium.
Sexton's poems in To Bedlam and Part Way
Back come out of such deep, painful elements of
the personality, that one's "literary opinions
scarcely seem to matter." "The experiences she
recounts are among the most harrowing that human
beings can undergo. . . . The poems fail to do
their subject justice. . . . Perhaps no poems
could."

2 WHITE, WILLIAM. "Lyrics Back to Sanity and Love."
       Prairie Schooner, XXXV (Spring, 1965), 3-4
           To Bedlam and Part Way Back records Sexton's
       battle against psychological disintegration;
       "the feeling runs deep," but the concern is too
       narrow. "Whether one feels Sexton's lines are
       therapy or artistry, for some they will be un-
       forgettable, for others 'different,' and for
       some a true poetic achievement."

A. Books--1962

None

B. Articles--1962

1 "Literature." Booklist, LIX (November 1, 1962), 200
           Briefly describes the contents of All My
       Pretty Ones.

2 BURKE, HERBERT. "Poetry." Library Journal,
       LXXXVII (October 1, 1962), 3457
           In All My Pretty Ones, Sexton extends the
       achievement of her earlier work. She speaks in
       several feminine voices "of a woman's loves and
       losses, of what morality means."

3 HEMLEY, CECIL. "A Return to Reality." Hudson Re-
       view, XV (Winter, 1962-1963), 612
           All My Pretty Ones deals primarily with death
       and Sexton's traumatized feelings. She "is a
       ruthlessly honest poet of great ability. Her
       book is both shocking and poignant."

4 SMITH, HAL. "Notes, Reviews and Speculations."
       Epoch, XII (Fall, 1962), 124-126
           All My Pretty Ones arouses less excitement
       because the reader had been initiated into

SMITH, HAL (cont.)
    Sexton's style by To Bedlam and Part Way Back.
    In this work "almost every poem shows a deepen-
    ing of inquiry and technique" in Sexton's abil-
    ity.

A. Books--1963

None

B. Articles--1963

1 BOGAN, LOUISE. "Verse." New Yorker, XXXIX (April
        27, 1963), 175-176
           Sexton's poems in All My Pretty Ones deal
        with the horrors of modern existence in a real-
        istic fashion. "She writes from the center of
        feminine experience with the direct and open
        feeling that women, always vulnerable, have been
        shy of expressing in recent years."

2 DAVISON, PETER. "New Poetry." Atlantic, CCX (Novem-
        ber, 1963), 87-88
           All My Pretty Ones shows a clear development
        in Sexton's poetry since To Bedlam and Part Way
        Back. Although she is frequently successful
        with the confessional mode, at times the arti-
        fice becomes too obvious in the "I" of the poem.

3 DICKEY, JAMES. "Dialogues With Themselves." New
        York Times (April 28, 1963), VII, p.50
           "It would be hard to find a writer who dwells
        more insistently on the pathetic and disgusting
        aspects of bodily experience." Sexton's atti-
        tude in All My Pretty Ones is "a curious com-
        pound of self-deprecatory cynicism and sentimen-
        tality-congratulating-itself-on-not-being-caught.

4   GUNN, THOM. "Poems and Books of Poems." Yale Re-
        view, LIII (October, 1963), 140-141
            In All My Pretty Ones, Sexton "has more con-
        trol over her material" than in To Bedlam and
        Part Way Back, but she does have difficulty in
        overcoming the influence of Robert Lowell. "It
        may be that she is most credible when she fic-
        tionalizes her experience: certainly she is at
        her best when she presents it indirectly or from
        a distance."

5   HOWARD, RICHARD. "Five Poets." Poetry, CI (March,
        1963), 413-414
            Sexton's All My Pretty Ones is harsh and bru-
        tal with all of the most terrible insights made
        glaringly public.

6   MILLS, RALPH J. "Four Voices in Recent American
        Poetry." Christian Scholar, XLVI (Winter,
        1963), 327-332
            In All My Pretty Ones, Sexton writes poetry
        with a brutal frankness on subjects of a highly
        personal nature. Her "poetry displays a stoic
        pessimism that occasionally lapses into morbid-
        ity, yet we cannot easily doubt the biting
        honesty of her intelligence or the truth to her
        life out of which she makes art." The subjects
        of family relationships and religion are dis-
        cussed.

7   ROSENTHAL, M. L. "Seven Voices." Reporter, XXVIII
        (January 3, 1963), 47-48
            Compares Sexton's All My Pretty Ones to Gins-
        berg's Kaddish and Levertov's The Jacob's Ladder.
        Sexton assumes that her theme of psychological
        breakdown is important, and "can 'afford' simply
        to show what she has been through and to use a
        certain restraint." Both Sexton and Ginsberg
        have yet to realize their full potential.

8   SIMMONS, CHARLES. "Poetry in Search of a Public."
       Saturday Review, XLVI (March 30, 1963), 47-48
          The poems in All My Pretty Ones speak simul-
       taneously of desperation and courage.

9   SMITH, W. J. "New Poetry." Harper's, CCXXVII (Sep-
       tember, 1963), 108, 110
          All My Pretty Ones is a "feminine version of
       Lowell's Life Studies." The poems are interest-
       ing because they treat most subjects honestly
       that most women writers would tend to avoid, but
       some of her writing would be better as prose.

10 STEPANCHEV, STEPHEN. "Eight Poets." Shenandoah,
       XIV (Spring, 1963), 58-65
          In All My Pretty Ones, Sexton is concerned
       with displaying the self in extreme situations.
       "Poetry serves her as both religion and psycho-
       analysis."

11 _____. "Chorus of Versemakers: A Mid-1963 Medley."
       New York Herald-Tribune (August 11, 1963), p.7
          In All My Pretty Ones, Sexton is "fluent and
       readable, and, like Robert Lowell, she knows the
       value of carefully chosen, objective detail in
       suggesting states of mind."

12 SWENSON, MAY. "Poetry of Three Women." Nation,
       CXCVI (February 23, 1963), 164-166
          All My Pretty Ones explores "other parts of
       the same psychological terrain" as To Bedlam
       and Part Way Back. Sexton's "method is as unin-
       hibited as entries in a diary or letter writing
       . . . the diction seems effortless, yet when we
       examine for form we find it solidly there and
       its expertness is a pleasurable thing in con-
       trast to the often merciless débridement taking
       place in the content."

13 TILLINGHAST, RICHARD. "Five Poets." Sewanee Re-
       view, LXXII (Summer, 1963), 510-513
          In All My Pretty Ones, Sexton is "too insis-
       tent upon dragging out her own problems for
       others to sympathize with." She has obviously
       been influenced by Robert Lowell and W. D. Snod-
       grass.

A. Books--1964

None

B. Articles--1964

1 FAIRFAX, JOHN. "More Than Are Dreamt Of." Poetry
       Review, LV (Winter, 1964), 249-251
          Selected Poems is an exciting book, filled
       with shockingly clear images. It is certainly
       one of the best contemporary collections of
       poems.

2 FURBANK, P. N. "Notes and Queries." Listener,
       LXXII (October 29, 1964), 689
          The poems in Selected Poems which speak
       "directly about agonizing change and shock . . .
       work by suggesting how much more there is, the
       superabundance of grim material reduced by
       fierce effort to order."

3 HORDER, JOHN. "Right Words, Wrong Words." Specta-
       tor, CCXIII (October 30, 1964), 580
          The poems in Selected Poems "aim 'high' and
       must be judged accordingly. They are not on a
       par with the late Sylvia Plath's last poems,
       which have a haunting quality Mrs. Sexton cannot
       quite emulate."

4 JONES, A. R. AND C. B. COX. "After the Tranquilized
       Fifties: Notes on Sylvia Plath and James Bald-
       win." Critical Quarterly, VI (Summer, 1964),
       107-122
           In "Sylvia's Death," Sexton shares an in-
       tensity of an emotional response to death with
       Sylvia Plath, a common "Dantesque community of
       the damned."

5 RICKS, CHRISTOPHER. "Beyond Gentility." New States-
       man, LXVIII (November 27, 1964), 842
           Although Sexton occasionally fails to rise
       above the factual in some poems in Selected
       Poems, she shows remarkable talent and poetic
       force.

A. Books--1965

None

B. Articles--1965

1 DODSWORTH, MARTIN. "Puzzlers." Encounter, XXIV
       (March, 1965), 86
           "Sexton's poems have been compared with
       Lowell's Life Studies, but their subject mat-
       ter--insanity, abortion, isolation and death--is
       more disturbing, and less well handled." Sexton
       has apparently suffered a great deal, but only
       occasionally does she manage to write of her
       suffering with excellence.

2 HAMILTON, IAN. "Poetry." London Magazine, IV
       (March, 1965), 87-88
           Anne Sexton's Selected Poems "show her to be
       the most promising American poet to have ap-
       peared here for some time. Although her poems

HAMILTON, IAN (cont.)
possess some flaws, "there is a remorseless accuracy of observation that carries its own sig-
nificance into what it seizes on."

3 HEANEY, SEAMUS. "Confessions and Histories." Out-
posts, 65 (Summer, 1965), 21-23
Anne Sexton's work in Selected Poems is near-
ly pure confessional poetry. She is able to
avoid the sensational and self-pitying extremes
of this mode and by courting disaster the poems
are "more exciting."

4 JONES, A. R. "Necessity and Freedom: The Poetry of
Robert Lowell, Sylvia Plath, and Anne Sexton."
Critical Quarterly, VI (Spring, 1965), 11-30
Deals with the major themes, poetic struc-
ture, perception, and attitude in Sexton's To
Bedlam and Part Way Back and All My Pretty Ones.
The persona of her poetry often represents "an
unstable and hysterical response to experience"
in a world of narrow perspectives.

5 "Pre-Fab Plastic and Passionate Ice-Picks." London
Times Literary Supplement (March 11, 1965),
p.196
Discusses the unconventional feminine theme,
the themes of tragedy and conflict, and mentions
the echo of Robert Lowell's Life Studies in Sexton's Selected Poems. "Miss Sexton's finest
poems draw the reader into her severe experience
through intensely following her need to control
them; this emerges as a passionate need to stop
them overwhelming her, and there is an edge of
something like hysteria in her work which never
allows her to make life tidy."

6 MARX, PATRICIA. "Interview With Anne Sexton." Hud-
      son Review, XVIII (Winter, 1965-1966), 560-570
         Sexton discusses her ideas on the poet's
      role, the psychological and other themes in her
      work, other poets that she likes and that have
      influenced her, and her response to critics.

7 MILLS, RALPH J. "A Note On the Personal Element in
      Recent American Poetry." Chicago Circle Studies,
      I (December, 1965), 7-11
         Mentions that Robert Lowell sees a resem-
      blance between Sexton's poetry and Russian real-
      ism.

8 _____. Contemporary American Poetry. New York:
      Random House, 1965, 218-234
         A general discussion of Sexton's works. Her
      poetry is "bold and impressive" and possesses
      an undoubted sense of honest revelation of the
      intuitive truth she feels. Comments on particu-
      lar poems in To Bedlam and Part Way Back and
      All My Pretty Ones.

9 SARGEANT, HOWARD. "Poetry Review." English, XVI
      (Spring, 1965), 154
         Review of Selected Poems.

10 STEPANCHEV, STEPHEN. American Poetry Since 1945.
      New York: Harper and Row, 1965, 5, 15
         Briefly comments on the autobiographical na-
      ture of Sexton's poetry.

A. Books—1966

None

B. Articles—1966

1 "Literature." Booklist, LXIII (December 1, 1966),
      401
         Briefly describes the contents of Live Or Die.

2 BURKE, HERBERT. "Poetry." Library Journal, XCI
      (September 15, 1966), 4126
         The poems in Live Or Die deal with important,
      formerly taboo, emotional subjects in a personal
      fashion.

3 CARRUTH, HAYDEN. "In Spite of Artifice." Hudson
      Review, XIX (Winter, 1966-1967), 698
         Live Or Die raises the question of the dif-
      ference between art and documentary. What Sex-
      ton "has written is strong, clear, rather
      simple, never repressed and yet never out of
      hand."

4 Kirkus Reviews, XXXIV (August 1, 1966), 798
         Describes the poems in Live Or Die.

5 "Books Ahead." National Observer (September 12,
      1966), p.23
         Notice of the publication of Live Or Die.

6 SLATER, JOSEPH. "Immortal Bard and Others." Satur-
      day Review, XLIX (December 31, 1966), 26
         Sexton's poems are produced "from the inner
      events of her life." Live Or Die is the
      chronicle of her return to psychological stabil-
      ity.

A   ABOUT ANNE SEXTON (1967)

A. Books--1967

None

B. Articles--1967

1 "Books in Brief." <u>Beloit Poetry Journal</u>, XVII (Summer, 1967), 34
      Sexton's <u>Live Or Die</u> deals with the "essential business of being a woman" and is "filled with affirmation."

2 BLACKBURN, T. R. "Three American Poets." <u>Poetry Review</u>, LVIII (Autumn, 1967), 255
      At times in <u>Live Or Die</u>, Sexton's insight comes from "the psychic fission of schizophrenia." Compares Sexton to Plath.

3 CANARROE, JOEL O. "Five Poets." <u>Shenandoah</u>, XVIII (Summer, 1967), 84-91
      The poems in <u>Live Or Die</u> explore the author's psychological state, but also illuminate our own. Nearly every poem deals in some way with death or dying. Sexton's work is well deserving of the Pulitzer Prize.

4 COX, C. B. "New Beasts for Old." <u>Spectator</u>, CCXIX (July 28, 1967), 106
      Sexton's self-exposure gives the persona of the poems in <u>Live Or Die</u> mixed qualities of pathos and absurdity. "Her success is that her tone can encompass such a range of unexpected emotions.

5 FEIN, RICHARD J. "The Demon of Anne Sexton." <u>English Record</u>, XVIII (October, 1967), 16-21
      Sexton's "poetry constantly faces us with the problem of how we disencumber ourselves from the

FEIN, RICHARD J. (cont.)
past, especially as the effort to disengage is
itself a deliberate involvement with the past,
all that has made us what we are." In To Bedlam and Part Way Back, All My Pretty Ones, and
Live Or Die, Sexton explores this theme in a
search for psychological redemption.

6 FIELDS, BEVERLY. "The Poetry of Anne Sexton" in
Poets in Progress. Ed. Edward Hungerford.
Evanston: Northwestern University Press, 1967,
250-285
The stated purpose of this criticism is to
avoid the biographical reading of Sexton's work,
assume that there is some aesthetic distance involved, and approach the poems through the re-
peated thematic patterns in To Bedlam and Part
Way Back and All My Pretty Ones. Extensive use
of quotations.

7 GREGORY, MICHAEL. "A First Book & A New One by
Anne Sexton." Trace, 64 (Spring, 1967), 131
Live Or Die suffers from an identification of
psychology and poetry. Only a few poems really
succeed. But "Anne Sexton is a fine poet.
Whether her problem is the imitative fallacy or
indefinite perception, I hope she resolves it
sufficiently to turn her work into poetry again."

8 LEGLER, PHILIP. "O Yellow Eye." Poetry, CX (May,
1967), 125-127
Live Or Die is a "brilliantly unified book."
Sexton's poetry has the power of portraying the
real terror of life.

9 _____. "Reviews." New Mexico Quarterly Review,
        XXXVII (Spring, 1967), 89-92
        Live Or Die retains some of the formal con-
    trol of Sexton's earlier work, "but the patterns
    are much freer, are more intrinsic to the emo-
    tional states the poems suggest." The only di-
    rect influence on this work is W. D. Snodgrass.

10 "Leaps and Plunges." London Times Literary Supple-
        ment (May 18, 1967), p.420
        Live Or Die is somewhat similar to the last
    poems of Sylvia Plath in stylistic conventions
    as well as theme. "It is impossible to read
    these poems without sensing a seething mass of
    self-indulgence behind them; not self-pity, cer-
    tainly, for the attention they ask is not pity
    but something like the gasp or shock the exhibi-
    tionist demands and expects. If we do not gasp,
    if we are not shocked, then we are left with
    little else."

11 MARTIN, GRAHAM. "Poets of a Savage Age." Listener,
        LXXVIII (July 6, 1967), 22
        Live Or Die continues the trend of poetry
    about psychological disintegration. This book
    is uneven and does not possess the poetic con-
    centration found in Lowell.

12 MC DONNELL, THOMAS P. "Light in a Dark Journey."
        America, CXVI (May 13, 1967), 729-731
        Sexton's poetry explores the realm of psychic
    disturbance and its fluctuations from discon-
    tinuity to order. "Anne Sexton is one of the
    few women writing poetry in the United States
    of whom it is possible to say that her woman-
    ness is totally at one with her poems. Dis-
    cusses To Bedlam and Part Way Back, All My
    Pretty Ones and Live Or Die.

13 PRESS, JOHN. "New Poems." Punch, CCLIII (July 5,
       1967), 34
          At her best in Live Or Die, Sexton gives
       "her poems a fine energy and disturbing, probing
       quality." But at her worst, the poems become
       embarrassing. In all, it is "an impressive
       volume," but more restraint is desired.

14 ROSENTHAL, M. L. The New Poets: American and Brit-
       ish Poetry Since World War II. New York: Oxford
       University Press, 1967, 131-138
          A discussion of Sexton's use of the confes-
       sional style, a comparison to Plath and Lowell,
       and comments on her ability to choose poetic
       patterns which tend to give the content of her
       poems a certain appropriateness.

15 ROSS, ALAN. "Poetry." London Magazine, VII (July,
       1967), 102-103
          The poems in Live Or Die are nothing but
       "despair, insanity, suicidal impulses, obsession
       with hunger for the sleep into oblivion, a day-
       dream of self-destruction."

16 SIMPSON, LOUIS. "Poetry." Harper's, CCXXXV
       (August, 1967), 90-91
          "Live Or Die . . . shows the limit of the
       method when it isn't strengthened by ideas."
       Although some of Sexton's earlier work was in-
       teresting, this volume seems little more than
       "mere self-dramatization."

17 SYMONS, JULIAN. "Moveable Feast." New Statesman,
       LXXIII (June 16, 1967), 849
          Some poems in Live Or Die suffer from lack of
       control, but where Sexton is in control there is
       real power in her expression of "agonies and
       illusions."

18 VENDLER, HELEN. "Recent American Poetry." Massa-
        chusetts Review, VIII (Summer, 1967), 547-548
            In Live Or Die, Sexton is frequently open to
        the charge of non-functional exhibitionism.

A. Books--1968

None

B. Articles--1968

1   DICKEY, JAMES. Babel to Byzantium: Poets and
        Poetry Now. New York: Farrar, Straus and
        Giroux, 1968, 133-134
            Reprints Dickey's review of To Bedlam and
        Part Way Back from Poetry.

2   MADDEN, CHARLES, ED. Talks With Authors. Carbon-
        dale: Southern Illinois University Press, 1968,
        151-179
            An interview with Sexton which took place on
        April 13, 1964. Sexton discusses "All My Pretty
        Ones," "The Division of Parts," "I Remember,"
        "Young," and "Flight." Preceded by a brief bio-
        graphical summary.

3   MORSE, S. F. "Poetry 1966." Contemporary Litera-
        ture, IX (Winter, 1968), 122-123
            Morse considers Live Or Die as better than
        All My Pretty Ones, but worse than To Bedlam and
        Part Way Back. Sexton should look for a new
        style and different content.

4   SARGEANT, HOWARD. "Poetry Review." English, XIX
        (Spring, 1968), 29
            Review of Live Or Die.

5 THORPE, MICHAEL. "Current Literature 1967." Eng-
      lish Studies, XLIV (June, 1968), 277
         Live Or Die ends "with embarrassing fatuity."
      Sexton is clearly not as able as Plath.

A. Books--1969

None

B. Articles--1969

1 BARNES, CLIVE. "The American Place Offers Mercy
      Street." New York Times (October 28, 1969),
      p.43
         Sexton's play is unsatisfactory. She fails
      to give the central character "dramatic signifi-
      cance" in a play that seems to dwindle to point-
      less autobiographical expostulation. "Sexton
      will have learned what she has to offer--a
      wreath of phrases, a sharpness of image. She
      may also have learned that the drama demands an-
      other dimension of involvement, more sustained
      than the quick thrust of poetry."

2 BERG, BEATRICE. "Oh, I Was Very Sick." New York
      Times (November 9, 1969), pp. 1, 7
         A biographical article based on an interview
      with Sexton. Discusses the background of Mercy
      Street, Sexton's response to the theatre and
      what she has learned from it, her personal his-
      tory, career as a poet, and the plot and theme
      of her play.

3 BURNS, GERALD. "Love and War Like They Are." South-
      west Review, LIV (Spring, 1969), 232-233
         With Sylvia Plath, Sexton practically in-
      vented the "Poem on the Gruesome Subject." Love
      Poems is her most consistent and best work.

4 Choice, VI (April, 1969), 218
> The poems in Love Poems are a twentieth cen-
> tury "feminine rendering" of a traditional
> theme.

5 DAVIS, DOUGLAS M. "New Reflection in Three Tomes of
'Love Poems.'" National Observer (March 17,
1969), p.21
> Sexton's concern with the theme of love in
> Love Poems is primarily with its physical nature.

6 DICKEY, WILLIAM. "A Place in the Country." Hudson
Review, XXII (Summer, 1969), 347-349
> Sexton's Love Poems is only a superficially
> serious book. She fails to relate her poems to
> the world, and they remain as expressions of
> self-indulgence. They "admit everything but a
> sense of relative importance; to permit all
> metaphors and then dismiss them as metaphor.
> The emotional consequence of such an admission
> is pathos."

7 HOWARD, RICHARD. Alone With America. New York:
Atheneum, 1969, 442-450
> Sexton has dared to speak of subjects that
> most have studiously avoided. Her work tends to
> destroy the normal conception of poetry by a
> therapeutic analysis of her psychological condi-
> tion. "Her's is the truth that cancels poetry,
> and her career as an artist an excruciating tra-
> jectory of self-destruction, so that it is by
> her failures in her own enterprise that she suc-
> ceeds, and by her success as an artist that she
> fails herself." Discusses To Bedlam and Part
> Way Back, All My Pretty Ones, Live Or Die, and a
> relationship to some of Roethke's ideas.

8 HOWES, VICTOR. "'Happy-making poet'--and Others."
      Christian Science Monitor (March 20, 1969), p.17
         Love Poems is not very interesting. "Perhaps
      unintentionally the confessional mode reveals
      that people with nothing to hide usually have
      little to confess."

9 KAUFFMANN, STANLEY. "On Theatre." New Republic,
      CLXI (November 22, 1969), 33
         Sexton's Mercy Street is a thoroughly unsat-
      isfying play and written less well than her
      poetry. "At present Mrs. Sexton's idea of a
      dramatic writing is to give alternate lines to
      different people."

10 KERR, WALTER. "A Woman Upon the Altar." New York
      Times (November 2, 1969), II, p.3
         Praises Sexton's use of ritual and the in-
      tensity of her theme. The rotating flashbacks
      produce "some riveting line images."

11 LASK, THOMAS. "Each In His Own Voice." New York
      Times (March 8, 1969), p.27
         The poems in Love Poems "read so easily that
      they might seem slight, but their impression
      remains after the words are silent." Sexton's
      matter-of-fact attitude is convincing. All of
      her poetry is an extension of the theme of psy-
      chological disintegration: the personal theme
      of finding reality in the world.

12 LEWIS, THEOPHILUS. "Mercy Street." America, CXXI
      (December 20, 1969), 622
         The direction and purpose of Sexton's play is
      unclear. It "swings backward and forward in
      time and leaves us precisely where we were at
      the start of the action."

13 MILLS, RALPH J. Creation's Very Self: On the Per-
        sonal Element in Recent American Poetry. Fort
        Worth: Texas Christian University, 1969, 33-34
            Comments on Sexton's "For All the Year of the
        Insane: A Prayer."

14 O'KEEFE, CAROLE. "Poetry." Library Journal, XCIV
        (March 15, 1969),
            Love Poems is "lyrical, frank and self-re-
        vealing." A recommended volume.

15 WALSH, CHAD. "Contemporary Poetry: Variety Is Its
        Vitality." Chicago Tribune (July 27, 1969),
        p.7
            Love Poems contains some of the most vital
        poetry of recent years.

A. Books--1970

None

B. Articles--1970

1 DURGNAT, RAYMOND. "Muses and Mechanisms." Poetry
        Review, LXI (Spring, 1970), 84
            Explains the reasons why this critic could
        not "fully . . . deploy my participation" in
        Sexton's Love Poems. However, some of the
        images that at first appeared clumsy gradually
        became more interesting.

2 FRASER, G. S. "New Poetry." Partisan Review,
        XXXVII (Fall, 1970), 299-300
            Love Poems is an interesting human document,
        which succeeds in arousing its intended effects.
        However it is not skillful poetry.

3 GULLANS, C. "Poetry and Subject Matter: From Hart
       Crane to Turner Cassity." Southern Review, VI
       (Spring, 1970), 497-498
          "These are not poems at all and I feel that I
       have, without right or desire, been made a
       third party to her conversations with her psy-
       chiatrist." "To pretend to speak" of Sexton's
       Live Or Die "as literature at all is simply
       silly."

4 HOWARD, RICHARD. "American Poetry 1969." Massachu-
       setts Review, XI (Autumn, 1970), 668
          Some of the poems in Love Poems are "of a
       typical Sextonish extravagance," but in others
       reality is particularized in such a way that it
       "nearly becomes myth."

5 "Presences and Processes." London Times Literary
       Supplement (March 12, 1970), p.279
          Love Poems has "a distinctive yet precarious
       strength." Her best poems are always ready to
       become like the worst. The confessional style
       Sexton employs prevents subtle expression in
       its search for authenticity.

6 "Craft Interview With Anne Sexton." New York Quar-
       terly, 3 (Summer, 1970), 8-12
          Sexton discusses her attitudes toward writ-
       ing, the public presentation of her work, and
       Lowell's influence on her poetry.

7 PHILLIPS, ROBERT. "The Bleeding Rose and the Bloom-
       ing Mouth." Modern Poetry Studies, I (1970),
       41-47
          The poems in Love Poems extend Sexton's use
       of the confessional mode and show that she has
       "abandoned" the thematic concern of her earlier

PHILLIPS, ROBERT (cont.)
work for a new interest dealing with the problems involved in love relationships. "The
book's general effect is of stoicism and self-
reliance rather than self-pity or dependence."

8 SPEARS, MONROE K. Dionysus and the City: Modernism
in Twentieth Century Poetry. New York: Oxford
University Press, 1970, 239, 263
Sexton has been influenced by Robert Lowell,
and, with Sylvia Plath's poetry, her work marks
"the full flowering of the open or experimental
movement."

9 VAN DUYN, MUNA. "Seven Women." Poetry, CXV
(March, 1970), 430-432
In works such as Sexton's Love Poems, the
poet is so self-absorbed that there is no possi-
bility for the reader to develop empathy with
the poetry or the poet.

A. Books--1971

None

B. Articles--1971

1 COXE, LOUIS. "Verse: A Muchness of Modernity."
New Republic, CLXV (October 16, 1971), 29-30
Though possessing numerous weak points,
Transformations shows a considerable change and
growth in Sexton's work. "Though the old angst
and terror are still there, a new (I think) ob-
jectivity--a distancing--has made another kind
of writing available" to Sexton.

2 KAMEEN, PAUL. Best Sellers, XXXI (November 1,
      1971), 348-349
         Sexton's Transformations universalizes
      Grimms' fairy tales in such a way as to add ma-
      turity to their themes and provide new insight,
      while simultaneously placing the mark of her
      own individual style upon them. This book marks
      a new turn in Sexton's work away from pure pro-
      fessional poetry to "subjects once or twice re-
      moved from direct internal experience."

3 KELVES, BARBARA. "The Art of Poetry XV: Anne Sex-
      ton." Paris Review, 52 (1971), 159-191
         After a brief biographical summary, Sexton
      discusses her start as a poet, the relationship
      between her poetry and psychological therapy,
      her family, Maxine Kumin, W. D. Snodgrass,
      Robert Lowell, Sylvia Plath, her own poetic de-
      velopment, and religion.

4 LEHMANN-HAUPT, CHRISTOPHER. "Grimms' Fairy Tales
      Retold." New York Times (September 27, 1971),
      p.33
         In Transformations, Sexton avoids the raw
      confession of first-person experience. "By
      using the artificial as the raw material of
      Transformations and working her way backwards
      to the immediacy of her personal vision, she
      draws her readers in more willingly, and there-
      by makes them more vulnerable to her sudden
      plunges into personal nightmare."

5 SMITH, JANET ADAM. "The Great God Wish." New York
      Review of Books (December 2, 1971), p.21
         Sexton recreates sixteen of the Grimms'
      fairy tales "with a bluntness and brutality that
      might well have startled the good brothers.

Index

The index is intended to provide access to
the information on Plath and Sexton contained
in the sections listing works about these
poets.   There are two separate parts of the
index, one on Plath and one on Sexton.   These
give the location of items by particular
authors who have written about Plath and Sexton and all of the entries in the bibliog-
raphies that specifically deal with their individual works.   The listing for each entry
is followed by a notation of where the work
can be found.   Thus, the first entry in the
Plath index reads, "Adams, P. 1971 B1." This
translates that in the section devoted to
writings about Sylvia Plath, under the year
1971, Phoebe Adams' work on Plath will be the
first entry listed under "Articles." All book
entries (those books which are exclusively
concerned with the author under consideration)
are given "A" numbers; all article entries
(which include not only articles, but reviews
and parts of books) are given "B" numbers.

Sylvia Plath: Index

SYLVIA PLATH: INDEX

SYLVIA PLATH: INDEX

SYLVIA PLATH: INDEX

SYLVIA PLATH: INDEX

SYLVIA PLATH: INDEX

SYLVIA PLATH: INDEX

SYLVIA PLATH: INDEX

Press, J.	1965 B11; 1967 B9
Pritchard, W.	1972 B27
Raven, S.	1963 B11
Richmond, L. J.	1971 B50
Rosenstein, H.	1972 B30
Rosenthal, L.	1971 B51
Rosenthal, M. L.	1965 B12; 1966 B16; 1967 B10-11
Ross, A.	1965 B13
Salamon, L. B.	1970 B11
Schmidt, M.	1972 B32
Scholes, R.	1971 B53
Sergeant, H.	1961 B5; 1962 B6; 1966 B17; 1971 B52
Sexton, A.	1966 B18
Simon, J.	1962 B7
Skelton, R.	1965 B14; 1971 B54
Smith, P.	1972 B33, 1973 B16
Smith, R.	1972 B34
Smith, W. J.	1966 B19
Spacks, P. M.	1972 B35

SYLVIA PLATH: INDEX

SYLVIA PLATH: INDEX

Williamson, A.   1970 B14

Winter Trees   1971 B3, B14, B34, B44,
                                   B47; 1972 A1, B3, B7-9, B13-
                                   14, B16, B18, B20, B23, B34-
                                   B36; 1973 A1, B1-3, B5, B9
                                   B12-13, B15

Zollman, S.   1969 B10

Anne Sexton: Index

ANNE SEXTON: INDEX

ANNE SEXTON: INDEX

ANNE SEXTON: INDEX